The Complete Ridin

BOOK 5

Driving

The Official Handbook of The
German National Equestri...

Kenilworth Press

© FN-Verlag der Deutschen Reiterlichen Vereinigung
GmbH approves this edition of 'Richtlinien für Reiten
und Fahren, Band V'

English Language edition © 1988
The Kenilworth Press Ltd
Addington
Buckingham MK18 2JR

Reprinted 1991, 1994

Translation by Christina Belton
Consultant Jane Kidd

Printed and bound in Great Britain by
Hillman Printers, Frome

British Library Cataloguing in Publication Data
A catalogue record for this book is available from the British Library.

ISBN 1-872082-05-X

Foreword

The previous seventeen editions of the German manual of riding contained a section on driving. However, owing to the increased interest in the sport, when the series of manuals was revised it was decided to devote a separate volume to this discipline.

It was proposed that the book should contain the principles of German driving based on the Achenbach system, and that it would be a revised and expanded version of the original.

It is hoped that the result will serve as a basis for training in riding and driving schools and in clubs; that it will be a useful guide for both instructors and students; and that driving enthusiasts will welcome this volume as they have previous ones.

Deutsche Reiterliche Vereinigung e.V.(FN)
Sports Division
Warendorf, Westphalia

Contents

SECTION TWO
Training of the Driving Horse in Single and Double Harness

Introduction

German driving is renowned the world over, not only because of the numerous successes achieved by German drivers in all branches of the sport, but also, and most importantly, because of the logical training system which it provides for both drivers and horses.

At the beginning of the last century, useful information on harnessing and driving technique had already been set down by the Bavarian *Ober-Bereiter* Franz-Xaver Schreiner and by *Stallmeister* Friedrich Hamelmann, yet it was not until 1922 that the system compiled by Benno von Achenbach received official recognition. This system was based on extensive studies, especially under the English teacher of driving, Howlett. To this day, Achenbach's book remains the authoritative work on driving.

In the modern industrial world the horse has become obsolete as a working animal, yet in the fields of sport and recreation it has enjoyed a revival on a scale which has exceeded all expectations. The sport of driving is represented by numerous national and international organisations, and there is talk of it becoming an Olympic sport.

However, driving also enjoys large-scale popularity as a leisure activity, and in this context ponies are becoming increasingly popular. Since many pleasure drivers and potential sporting drivers lack the experience in handling horses which was once taken for granted – fitting and putting on harness, deciding on the most suitable harness, putting to and adjusting the harness to keep wear and tear to the minimum, and general driving techniques – thorough, systematic training is imperative.

This training should not be limited to 'drills', as is often thought, although these drills are necessary for handling a team properly. The main aim is to produce a driver who will not, through ignorance, cause suffering and injury to his horse, or place himself and other road users at risk as a result of bad harnessing and driving technique.

SECTION ONE

Basic Training of the Driver: Single Turnouts and Pairs

1. Prerequisites for Successful Training

1(1) The Instructor

Only a person who has achieved practical as well as theoretical mastery of a subject can teach it. As well as knowledge of his subject, the instructor must have teaching ability, strength of character, and qualities of leadership. The instruction must follow a systematic progression and be comprehensive and varied. Explanations must be clear and suited to the level of understanding of the pupils.

In Germany, professional instructors are expected to have given proof of their skills and knowledge by passing the relevant examination, which has been in existence and has been recognised by the state since 1927. The syllabus for this and other examinations can be found in the Training and Examinations Schedule (*Ausbildungs- und Prüfungs-Ordnung* or APO), obtainable from the German National Federation, the *Deutsche Reiterliche Vereinigung e.V. (FN)*, 4410 Warendorf, West Germany.

1(2) Facilities for Training and the Training Schedule

Driving training can be divided into the following sections:
☐ Theory.
☐ Theoretical-cum-practical.
☐ Practical only.
In the theoretical part the student is acquainted with the principles of the Achenbach system of driving, theoretical horse knowledge, the highway code and other relevant regulations. This part should be conducted in a classroom or, if the weather is suitable, outdoors in a quiet place

where there is nothing to disturb the pupil's concentration. The theoretical-cum-practical section comprises the following: harness, putting to and taking out, grooming and horse management, and position of the hands and handling the reins on the 'driving apparatus'. The theory is closely combined with practical demonstration. Classrooms, tack rooms, corridors or harness rooms can be used for this section.

Quiet roads or training grounds are the best places for the purely practical part of the training. Training grounds must not be too small – 50 x 50m should be the minimum. Later training and competition preparation takes place on specially designed arenas of 100 x 40m.

The ground in the training area should be as level as possible and not too deep. Tarmac or paved areas should be avoided as far as possible because of the risk of horses slipping and because of the strain on their legs.

Only when the student is proficient in handling the turnout should occasional driving in traffic be introduced. In contrast to driving training in days gone by, present-day training on the roads should be restricted to a few hours only. In modern fast-moving traffic a horse and cart almost always proves a nuisance and a source of danger. The most suitable routes for driving are by-roads and tracks through fields and woodland – with respect, of course, for the relevant laws and regulations.

The best way to start teaching driving is to begin with the theoretical and practical-cum-theoretical parts. The instructor can train eight to twelve pupils at the same time, especially when using the driving apparatus and other training aids.

To save wear and tear on the horses and to help prevent accidents, it is a good idea not to begin the practical training until the student has mastered the most important rein holds. During this phase the number of students should be strictly limited, since the instructor can watch only one at a time. If more than one turnout is available, a suitably qualified assistant – for example a holder of the Certificate of Competence in Driving (*Fahrwart-Prüfung*) – can be enlisted to accompany another turnout, having first been briefed by the instructor. Larger groups of pupils must be divided up and should busy themselves with exercises on the driving apparatus while awaiting their turn to drive.

Since to begin with the practical training of the beginner takes place only in walk, the instructor should take the reins from time to time and drive the horses at a trot to prevent them from 'going to sleep', falling apart, or becoming frisky through boredom.

Throughout the course, theoretical and practical tuition should be alternated so as to retain the student's interest and not to overtax him in any one sphere.

1(3) The Principles of the Achenbach System of Driving

The principal merits of the Achenbach system lie in:

☐ Its rules for harness, harnessing up and putting to, which are based on safety and respect for the well-being of the horses.

☐ Its clear instructions for a practical, safe method of driving which is also easy on the horses, in that turns are conducted by lengthening the outside rein. Also, all the reins are held permanently in the left hand, leaving the right hand free for other activities (e.g. braking). The method of holding the reins does not have to be re-learned when up-grading from single turnouts to multiples since it is the same.

☐ Its crossed reins, which can, through skilful handling and adjustment of the coupling buckles, compensate for different temperaments and make the horses do the same amount of work, thus permitting a rational exploitation of horse power. An additional factor which contributes to the success of this type of rein handling is the fixed splinter bar used on the carriage (see section 3.3).

However, the advantages of the Achenbach system of

14

driving only apply if the whip, as the driver is known, has learnt to 'see' and 'think'. Even the best system will be rendered worthless by the mechanical application of rein-handling techniques learnt without reasoning or feeling, and failure to take into account and to balance out the differences between individual horses when fitting harness and bridles, and when putting to.

1(4) The Driver's Dress and Equipment

Unlike the rider, the driver does not require any special clothing, though he should wear clothes suitable for working with horses – any tough, easily maintained clothing will do, provided it allows the necessary freedom of movement. If he wears baggy, flapping clothes, the driver runs the risk of their being caught on the pole, splinter bar, wheel hub or brake and of being dragged. Shoes must be sturdy and not easily pulled off. Sandals and lightweight shoes do not protect the foot from injuries from horses' hooves or carriage wheels. It is a good idea to wear fairly roomy leather gloves.

In sporting driving and competitions the driver and passenger or groom dress according to the type of competition, the vehicle and the harness. More details can be found in the German book of general competition regulations, the *Leistungs-Prüfungs-Ordnung* or LPO, or in the schedule for the competition in question.

An essential part of the driver's equipment in all circumstances is a suitable whip. The whip takes the place of the rider's legs, and is also used to give traffic signals. The 'apron' protects the driver's legs down to just below the knee from being soiled by the greased reins. It also prevents the ends of the reins falling between the driver's legs. The apron may consist of a small woollen blanket, or it may be made of thick drill or linen and be tailored to fit. In sporting driving and competitions the colour should tone in with that of the vehicle and seat cushions.

2. Harness and Equipment for the Horse

2(1) Types of Harness

There are two types of harness, *breastcollar harness* and *full collar harness* (*collar harness*). Both types have their advantages and disadvantages.

Breastcollar harness is lighter than full collar harness and is more easily interchangeable between horses. Its disadvantage is that it presses on the shoulder joint and so restricts the horse's freedom of movement, and in heavy draught it narrows the horse's chest.

Full collar harness fits the shape of the horse's neck and chest better, and even in heavy draught it does not restrict the horse's freedom of movement or his breathing. However, because of its rigidity, it must be correctly and individually fitted for each horse. Changes in the condition of the horse, for example due to feeding or fitness, will necessitate restuffing the collar.

The difference between the two kinds of harness is also reflected in the price. Breastcollar harness can be made up and bought considerably more cheaply than its full collar equivalent.

Full collar harness is more common in sporting driving, and goes with a 'town turnout'. Breastcollar harness goes with a 'country turnout' or 'Jucker' (Hungarian) turnout.

There is no significant difference between the bridle and reins used with a breastcollar harness and those used with full collar.

2(2) Bridle and Bits

A driving bridle is made up of various parts as shown in the illustrations on pages 18-19.

16

The browband must be long enough not to pull the headpiece forward so that it rubs against the ears. The blinkers – also known as winkers or blinders – are not as essential on single turnouts as they are with pairs and teams, when they prevent the horses seeing the whip coming. Without them, keen horses will not relax, but will use the driver's and groom's every movement as an excuse to become more and more excited. On the other hand, lazy, cunning horses will take advantage of the fact that they can see the driver to wait until the whip is raised before going into the traces. With pairs and teams it is not possible to drive correctly, in a manner designed to preserve the horses and with correct distribution of the work, if the horses are not wearing blinkers. Rarely are two or more horses so alike in temperament and other characteristics, or endowed with such good temperaments, that these problems do not arise.

Fitting and putting on a driving bridle requires special care because of the blinkers. Blinkers are made of leather and are basically square, with rounded corners and with a slight outward bulge on a level with the horse's eyes. They owe their rigidity to a metal or plastic plate sewn into them. Correctly fitted blinkers point slightly outwards, and are held in this position by the winker stays, which are strips of strong leather, sometimes padded underneath, sewn on to the blinkers at one end and fastened at the other to a buckle attached to the top of the headpiece between the ears. The blinkers must be attached to the cheekpiece throughout their length. It is incorrect for the top part, near the buckle, not to be attached, because this part can bend inwards and press against the horse's eyebrow and temple.

The outward bulge referred to above must be in the upper third of the blinker so as to leave enough space for the eye. Blinkers which are too close can cause the horse's eyelashes to press against his eye and cause considerable pain. Blinkers which are too small or made of soft or floppy leather are useless.

Driving bridle.

1 Headpiece
2 'D' for attachment of bearing rein drop (bridoon hanger)
3 Rosette
4 Throatlatch
5 Cheekpiece
6 Noseband
7 Winker, blinker or blinder
8 Browband
9 Face drop (facepiece)
10 Winker stay buckle
11 Winker stay
12 Curb hook
13 Liverpool bit

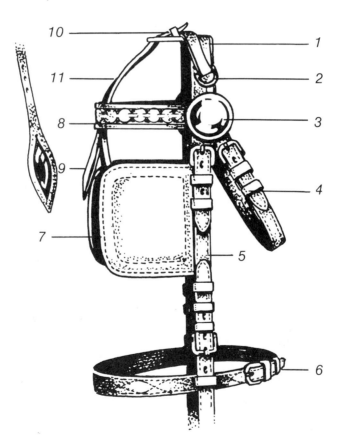

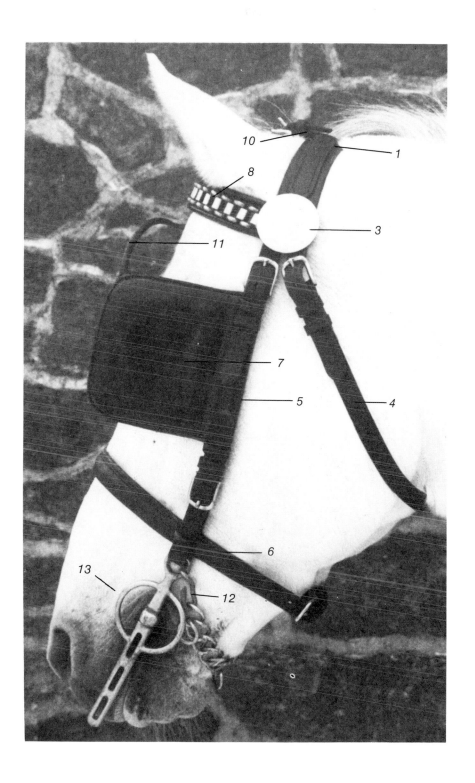

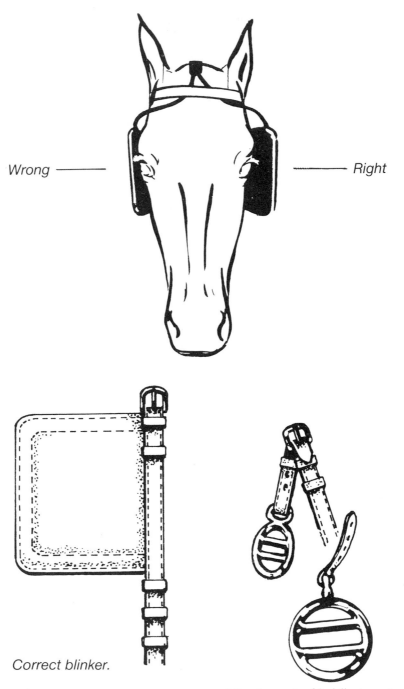

Wrong ———

——— Right

Correct blinker.

Attachment of bridle terret
(lead rein drop)
to throatlatch.

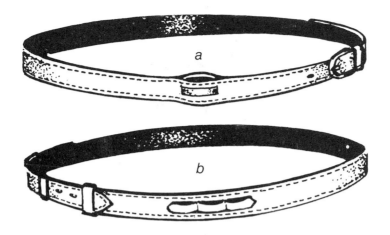

Correct noseband:
(a) outside
(b) inside

Another peculiarity of the driving bridle is the way in which the noseband is fastened. The main function of the noseband on a driving bridle is not to keep the horse's mouth shut but to transfer part of the action of the bit on to the bridge of the horse's nose. This can only be achieved if the noseband is attached to the cheekpieces in such a way that they cannot slide back along it. It must also be possible to alter the position of the noseband in relation to the cheekpieces. The design shown in the illustration fulfils these requirements.

The 'face drops' which hang below the browband are used with pairs and multiples to make all the horses look alike from the front. The rosettes at the junctions between the browband and the cheekpieces are also without any functional significance. On pairs and multiples the rosettes should be on the outside only, so as not to cause injury to the adjacent horse. It is possible to distinguish between the bridles of the off and near horses by the position of the rosette on each.

The little rings on the side of the headpiece are for the bearing rein, which may be used at some point in the horse's dressage training. They should not be used

21

for attaching the bridle terret when driving multiples. The bridle terret, or lead rein drop, is on a leather strap which is buckled into the throatlatch buckle.*

Stars and such like paraphernalia hanging loose from the bridle are pointless and dangerous – they can cause injury to both man and horse.

The most useful bits for driving are:

□ Double ring (Wilson) snaffles (jointed bits).
□ Curbs.
□ Curbs with snaffle (jointed) mouthpieces.

Snaffles are used with breastcollar harness and curbs with full collar. However, the primary considerations in choosing a bit should be the shape of the mouth, the individual characteristics of the horse and its level of training.

As a rule, breastcollar harness, with its Hungarian variation, 'Jucker' harness, is used where there is plenty of space, and for travelling at speed with little regard for collection. The snaffle used with breastcollar harness consists of one fixed and one loose or 'floating' ring, and for this reason is known as a 'double ring snaffle' (Wilson snaffle). By buckling the rein to both or just one ring the action of the bit can be varied from mild to severe. With Hungarian harness a double ring snaffle with indentations around the rings is used (Esterházy Jucker snaffle).

Full collar harness (town turnout) is used primarily for dressage-style driving in restricted areas, with part of the work being carried out at collected gaits. The various curb bits are used for this purpose.

Some curb bits have a sliding cheek, that is the mouthpiece can be slid a little way up or down the cheekpiece. The advantage lies in the fact that the bit changes its position whenever the horse moves his mouth, which is useful with hard-mouthed horses.

---

*Fixed terrets attached to the rosettes can also be used, though they are not as good.

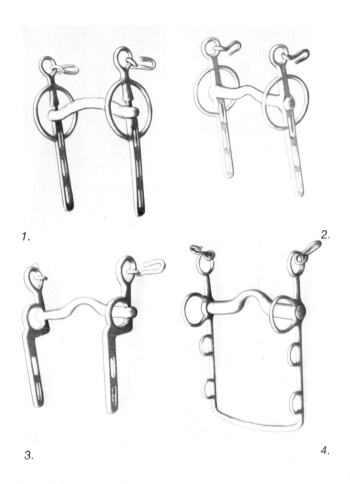

1.

2.

3.

4.

Permitted bits for driving competitions in Germany

With full collar harness:

1 *Slide-cheek Liverpool.*
2 *Fixed-cheek Liverpool with port. Any ports, including Segundo ports, are permitted with all curb bits.*
3 *Elbow bit (army reversible, angle-cheek Pelham) with or without bottom cross bar, slide cheek, or fixed cheek, and with any port.*
4 *Gig bit or Tilbury.*

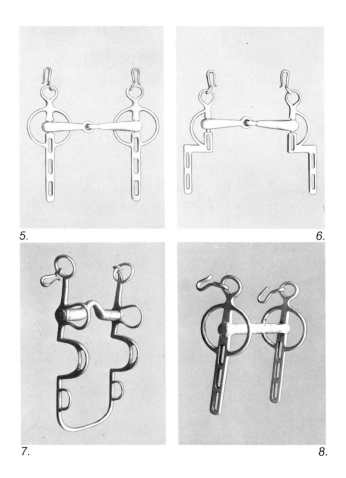

5 Liverpool, with jointed mouthpiece and curb chain.
6 Elbow bit (army reversible, angle-cheek Pelham), with
   jointed mouthpiece and curb chain.
7 Buxton.
8 Liverpool, with serrated and smooth straight-bar
   mouthpiece.

However, it does have the disadvantage that it can easily
cause injury to the lips.
    Curb bits used for driving – which, unlike some used

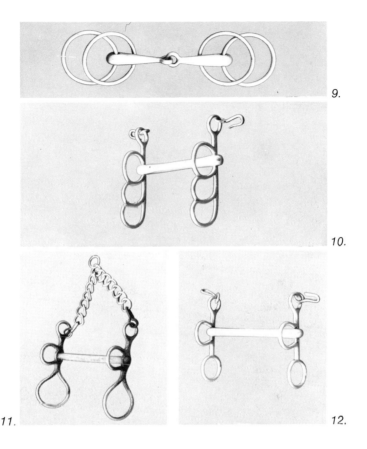

9.

10.

11.

12.

With breastcollar harness:

9 *Double ring (Wilson) snaffle, also with indented outer ring (Esterhazy Jucker snaffle).*
10 *11, 12 Types of Pelham (10 butterfly Pelham, 'knuckle duster'), (11, 12 globe-cheek Pelham), also permitted with jointed mouthpieces.*

All driving curbs and Pelhams to be fitted with curb chains as shown in illustration 11.

for riding, are not accompanied by a bridoon – may have higher ports (Howlett) or ports which are wider at the top (Segundo).

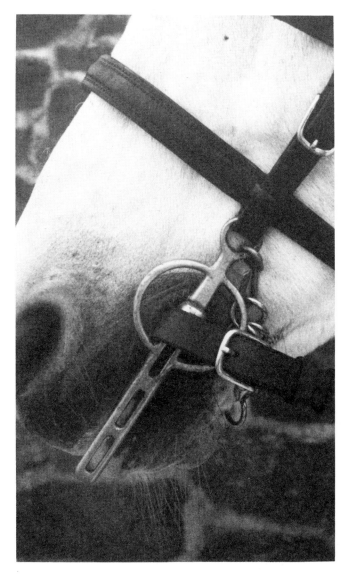

Rough cheek (mild) rein setting on a Liverpool bit.

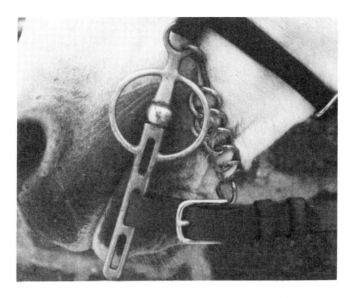

Middle bar (severe) rein setting on a Liverpool bit.

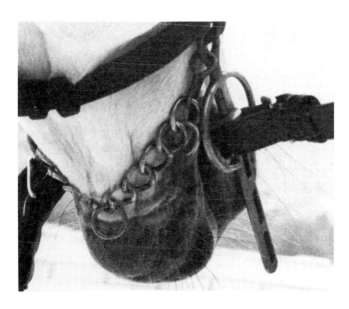

Method of attaching the inside rein.

27

The lever action of the curb is based on the resistance produced by the curb chain. The severity of the action can be adjusted by buckling the reins to different 'slots' in the cheeks. The least amount of leverage, and so the mildest action, is obtained by buckling the reins around the branches of the bit just below the mouthpiece ('rough cheek' position).

Any bit, but particularly a curb, must be fitted with utmost care. Since the shape of the jaw and the size of the mouth is different in every horse, bits must always be fitted individually. Bits recommended by dealers and strangers as being 'really gentle' can have a very severe action on some horses' mouths. This is often the case with bits which have a curved mouthpiece, which is supposed to be the same shape as the horse's mouth. The most important thing to look for in a bit is that it is the correct width for the horse's mouth and that it lies correctly on the lower jaw. As for that part which is outside the horse's mouth, the upper branch of the cheek must be bent outwards so that the bridle's cheekpiece billet does not rub the horse.

The curb hooks, for the curb chain, must curve outwards and hang down as far as the mouthpiece. Correct bitting depends on the curb hooks being bent correctly. Misshapen curb hooks, or hooks fitted incorrectly (for example, a right hook on the left side of the bit), cause injury to the horse's mouth.

In contrast to a curb bit used on a riding horse, that used on a driving horse sometimes has the opening of the curb hook at the back.* In the case of a riding horse the aim is to avoid getting the bridoon caught on the hooks; with a driving horse, it is to avoid the hooks being caught up on the adjacent horse, the pole or other parts of harness or carriage underneath the horse's head.

---

* In the photographs (pages 18-27) the opening is at the front. In Britain curb hooks on both riding and driving horses are usually fitted with the opening at the back.

2(3) Breastcollar Harness for Singles and Pairs

Single breastcollar harness

Single breastcollar harness consists of a breastcollar and a saddle or pad. The main difference between single and pair or team harness is that with single harness there is a different arrangement for attaching the shafts to the pad, and the pad is more stoutly constructed.

The breastcollar itself is broad and padded, and is suspended from a neck strap. The height of the breastcollar is adjusted by means of a buckle, or buckles, on the neckstrap. Narrow breastcollars are incorrect because they cut into the chest and cause the horse pain when he is pulling. The top part of the neck strap is wider and may be padded. It lies on the neck, just in front of the withers and a little behind the perpendicular.

The sides of the breastcollar are joined to the traces. The best method is to sew the traces on to the breastcollar, but the drawback is that the length of the traces cannot then be adjusted and, if a trace breaks, the whole collar has to be consigned to the saddler's for repair.

These drawbacks are avoided if the traces are buckled on to the collar. The buckle must lie in front of the pad. If this method is used, the shafts on the vehicle must not be too narrow or the trace buckle may rub against the horse's side. The buckle must not be on the rear third of the trace, because the tail hairs will catch on it and be pulled out. There is also the risk that the buckle will touch the horse's hind leg and make him kick.

In single harness the saddle, which is called a pad in pair and team harness, is wider and heavier because it has to take the weight of the shafts.

As with a riding saddle, the part of the pad which sits on the horse's back is built on a rigid tree made of metal, leather or a synthetic material. The sides are well padded so that the top does not rest on the withers. The bottom part of the pad consists of a girth, which should not be

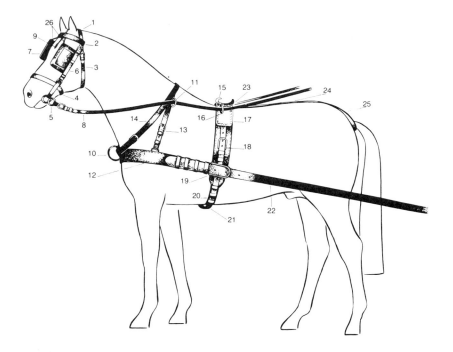

Breastcollar pair harness.

1 Headpiece with winker stay buckle
2 Browband
3 Throatlatch
4 Noseband
5 Double ring (Wilson) snaffle
6 Cheekpiece
7 Blinker/winker
8 Rein
9 Face drop
10 Pole strap ring
11 Rein terret
12 Breastcollar
13 Neck strap
14 Yoke strap (passes through pole strap ring)
15 Bearing hooks
16 Terret
17 Pad
18 Point strap
19 Trace tug buckle
20 Girth
21 (False) bellyband
22 Trace
23 Crupper 'D'
24 Backstrap
25 Crupper dock
26 Winker stays

too narrow. For maximum safety the back band should be made out of a single piece of leather. It is not attached to the top part of the saddle but is free to slide through it from side to side. This enables it to absorb sideways movements of the vehicle, and reduces the jarring on the horse's back.

Two different kinds of tug are in use, depending on the type of vehicle. With four-wheeled vehicles only, the actual weight of the shafts is borne by the tugs. With two-wheeled vehicles there is a lot of strain on the saddle and in particular on the tugs, especially when the vehicle is badly balanced. The tugs for a four-wheeled vehicle – French Tilbury tugs – consist of a metal cup, to the top of which is attached the belly band. Tugs for a two-wheeled vehicle (open tugs) consist of heavy-duty loops made of several layers of leather sewn together, and connected by the belly band.

The crupper, consisting of a back strap and dock, is attached to a 'D' ring on the back of the saddle. The protruding point of the strap on the back band should

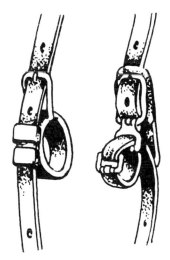

For single turnouts.

Left: Leather 'open' tug for two-wheeled vehicle.
Right: Metal 'French Tilbury tug' for a four-wheeled vehicle.

31

be secured, and the buckle part designed and constructed to ensure that the reins cannot become caught on it. The back band must be sewn on to the dock: buckles between the two would become caught on the tail hairs, pulling them out. The part of the dock which lies underneath the dock of the horse's tail is padded so that the tail is raised, which makes it difficult for the horse to clamp down on the reins and trap them. The purpose of the crupper is to keep the saddle in its correct position behind the withers. This is particularly important with single turnouts because the saddle – together with the girth and belly band – acts as a brake.

Crupper

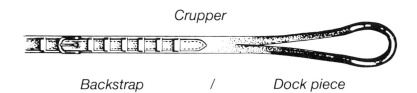

Backstrap / *Dock piece*

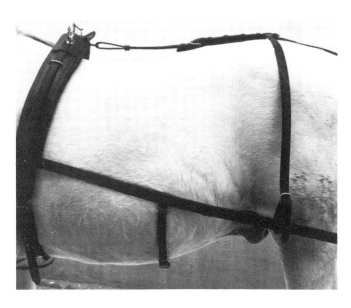

Correct position of the trace bearer: behind the hip bone and not 'breaking the draught' (the trace remains straight).

In hilly areas, or for increased safety, a breeching can be used with a single harness. If no breeching is fitted, a kicking strap should be used. The kicking strap passes through a loop on the rear third of the crupper back strap and attaches at the sides to the 'Ds' provided for this purpose on the shafts. It restricts the upward movement of the croup (bucking and kicking) and so prevents accidents. It also acts as a trace bearer and prevents the traces flapping against the horse's hind legs. Terrets for the reins to pass through are fixed to the sides of the saddle at the top and to the neck strap. Between the two terrets on the saddle is a bearing hook. This serves as a point of attachment for the bearing rein, which is sometimes used in training driving horses.

Pair breastcollar harness

Pair harness differs from single harness in that a steel 'D' for the pole strap is sewn on to the breastcollar, and the saddle, known as a 'pad', is of lighter construction.

The pole strap rings are positioned slightly to the inside (pole side) of the collar, and the near and off side collars can be told apart by the position of the rings. The rings are off-centre to accommodate the sideways pull of the pole straps which connect the collar to the pole. If they were central, the collar would be pulled sideways.

Additional support for the breastcollar can be provided in the form of an extra neck strap (yoke strap) running from the top of the first, and round the front of the chest through the pole strap ring. This extra strap is particularly useful on team harness, because of the additional weight of the lead bars on the wheelers' collars.

Instead of a back band there is a fixed strap on each side of the pad. This strap and the belly band (not the girth, which holds the pad in position), serve to keep the traces in their correct position, preventing them from riding up or down and restricting their sideways movement.

The hame tug buckle has a 'D' at the top for the attachment of the pad strap, and one at the bottom for the belly band. In double harness the near (left) horse's belly band fastens on the near side and that of the off (right) horse on the off side, so that the driver can always reach the buckles, even when the horses are attached to the carriage.

Since the lightweight construction of double harness makes it unsuitable for even temporary use as single harness, the rein terret on the inside of the neck strap may be left off. The use of such a terret would cause the neck strap to be drawn constantly towards the other horse.

It is advisable to use a breeching in hilly areas.

There is no kicking strap on pair harness. If the length of the pole straps and traces is correctly adjusted, a trace bearer is also unnecessary. Other details of breastcollar pair harness are the same as for single harness.

The pole straps are an essential part of pair harness. They serve to steer the pole and are also used for braking and pushing the vehicle backwards. Pole straps are made of two layers of bent leather sewn together. They run from the pole strap rings on the breastcollars to the pole head, and do up with a buckle fastening. Pole straps, and not pole chains, should always be used with breastcollar harness. Pole chains spoil the general impression since they do not fit in with the style of the harness.

Since horses tend to line up their inner side with the pole, the fact that the hindquarters are wider than the forehand means that the outside hindquarter sticks out and is further forward, and so further away from the splinter bar, than the inside one. For this reason the outside trace should be 2cm longer than the inside. Since

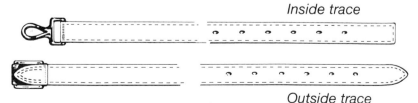

Inside trace

Outside trace

Different methods of attaching the trace to the swingle tree.

the inside trace rubs against the pole and becomes covered in sweat, it is a good idea always to use the same trace on the inside, and to keep the smarter one for the outside. So that the inside and outside traces can be more easily distinguished from each other, the end of the shorter inside trace is straight, while the outside one is pointed.

2(4) Full Collar Harness for Singles and Pairs

Full collar harness for single turnout

The horse's strength is exploited to best effect by the full collar, which enables him to pull heavier loads. Full collars are more difficult to fit than breastcollars. Changes in the amount of muscle and fat carried by the horse affect the fit of the collar. Small changes can be compensated for by buckling a pad underneath the collar, but more significant variations necessitate the whole collar being reshaped and restuffed by the saddler.

Collar harness for a single turnout consists of the collar, the saddle and the traces. The collar is pear shaped to give an anatomically correct fit on the shoulders, the top of the neck in front of the withers and the chest. The collar must be sufficiently well padded to prevent the hame lugs, under any circumstances, rubbing the shoulders.

The hames, which lie on top of the padded part of the collar, must be made of high quality material because they have to take a great deal of strain. The hames are held together by the hame strap at the top of the collar, which is protected by a little leather 'hat' to prevent water penetrating the stuffing. On single harness the buckle of the hame strap points to the left and the point of the strap to the right. Every driving person knows that, thanks to this rule, in an emergency the hame strap can easily be undone from the near side to release the horse from the shafts. A similar rule applies for pairs and teams: the hame straps are undone from the outside, that is, the left horse's strap from the left and the right horse's strap from the right. On single harness there is a hook at the bottom of the hames on each side. The hame chain, which has a little ring for the false martingale, is attached to these hooks.

The hame tug is attached to the hames by two inter-locking closed steel rings. They should not be detachable nor should they have specially designed or spring clips on the end. Serious accidents have been caused by hame tugs coming off.

On the top third of the hames are the rein terrets. On single harness it is not necessary for them to move up and down, but they should be able to move backwards and forwards so that they are less susceptible to breakage when the harness is being transported or stored.

The hame tug buckles, at the end of the hame tugs, should be as flat as possible so as not to take up space between the shafts.

The traces attach to the hame tug buckles. The length is adjusted by some five oval-shaped holes at the end of the trace, the middle (third) hole being about 35cm from the end. At the rear end of the trace is a metal running loop with a little leather tab or hand piece. This is used to attach the trace to the vehicle (swingle tree or splinter bar).* On single harness the traces are of equal length.

To help keep it in position at fast paces, the collar is connected to the girth of the saddle by a false martingale, which is passed through the ring on the hame chain and round the whole of the bottom of the collar. A space is left in the padding into which the martingale fits, so that it does not gall the horse's chest. The saddle used with full collar harness is constructed in the same way as that used with breastcollar harness, and is judged by the same criteria. The same applies to the kicking strap and the breeching.

---

* In Britain most single harness traces have a 'crew hole' at the end which fastens on to the trace hook on the end of the swingle tree or splinter bar.

Collar harness for single turnout, but without breeching or kicking strap which should be available for use with single harness.
Below: Collar harness for a pair.

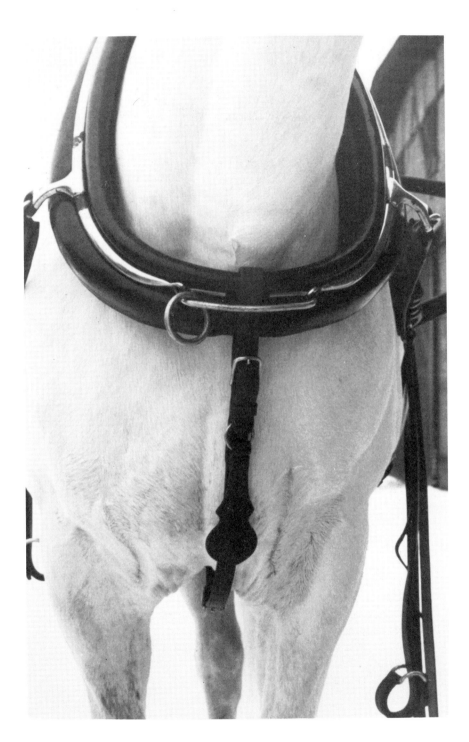

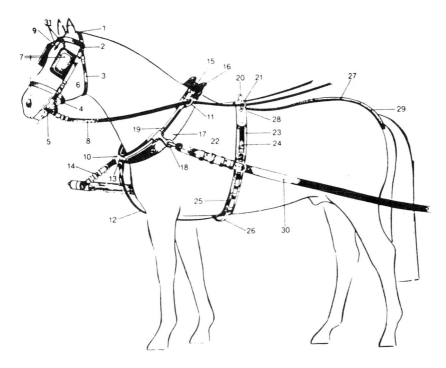

Collar harness for pairs.

1 Headpiece with winker stay buckle	17 Collar
2 Browband	18 Hame draught eye
3 Throatlatch	19 Hames
4 Noseband	20 Bearing hook
5 Bit	21 Terret
6 Cheekpiece	22 Hame tug
7 Blinker	23 Pad
8 Rein	24 Point strap
9 Face drop	25 Girth
10 Kidney link ring	26 False belly band
11 Rein terret	27 Crupper backstrap
12 False martingale	28 Crupper 'D' ring
13 Kidney link	29 Crupper dock piece
14 Pole strap	30 Trace
15 Hame strap	31 Winker stays
16 Neck of collar	

Left: Kidney link and kidney link ring on pair collar harness.

Collar harness for pairs

Pair collar harness differs from single harness in the following respects:

☐ The hames are connected at the bottom with a kidney link.

☐ The pole strap ring is on the kidney link.

☐ The rein terrets fixed to the hames move up and down on double harness. If they were rigid, each horse would be jerked in the mouth by his neighbour's rein with every movement of the shoulder.

☐ The hame tugs attached to the hames are longer than those used for single harness, and the hame tug buckles have attachment points to which the pad strap and belly band – or belly band strap – are sewn or buckled.

☐ The outside trace is 2cm longer than the inside one, for the same reasons as for breastcollar harness.

☐ There is no need for a rosette on the inside of the bridles.

☐ Instead of a saddle, a lightweight pad, without tugs, is used.

☐ There is no kicking strap. The use of a breeching is advisable in hilly country.

The other parts, such as the crupper and so on, are of the same design and are used in the same way as with single breastcollar harness.

2(5) Reins for Single Turnouts and Pairs

The construction of the reins is of the utmost importance for the whip, the passengers and the horse. Reins must be made from best quality materials, with no weak points or other sources of danger. The reins must be kept safe by constant care and inspection.

With pairs and teams, the reins have an additional function. Their design, and the adjustment on the couplings, mean that they not only serve to steer the horses, but also allow the work to be shared equally and for different temperaments to be accommodated.

Single reins

Single reins consist of two separate pieces, each about 4.50m long. (This measurement applies to a full-sized horse and carriage. For ponies the length is reduced accordingly.) They have billets at the front for attaching them to the bit, and there is a buckle at the other end of them, with which to buckle them together. New reins should be at least 25mm wide. With daily use they wear down and become narrower.

Since it would be very expensive to make each rein out of a single piece of leather, there is a splice approximately in the middle. Obviously, the two ends should lie flat on top of each other at the join and should offer no resistance when sliding through the terrets.

At sporting events and competitions, leather reins are used. Leather reins with webbing hand parts have proved successful for everyday driving. The webbing part should start at least two thirds of the way down the rein so that the splice is not damaged by rubbing against the pad. Reins made entirely of webbing are not recommended since they wear excessively at the points where they pass through the terrets, and become both unsafe and unsightly.

Pair reins

Pair reins are designed with couplings, so that one rein acts on two horses. These coupling reins are crossed between horses, and therefore pair reins have become known as 'cross reins'.

Pair reins need to be both safe and effective. Apart from a few home-made variations, which do not as a rule fulfil these requirements, there are two kinds of reins in general use today:

☐ The improved 'English reins', developed by Benno von Achenbach in 1922 and known as 'Achenbach reins'.
☐ The Viennese or Hungarian reins.

The essential characteristics of these reins are listed below. Both types of rein overcome the problems of earlier

41

Measurements for crossed (Achenbach) reins.

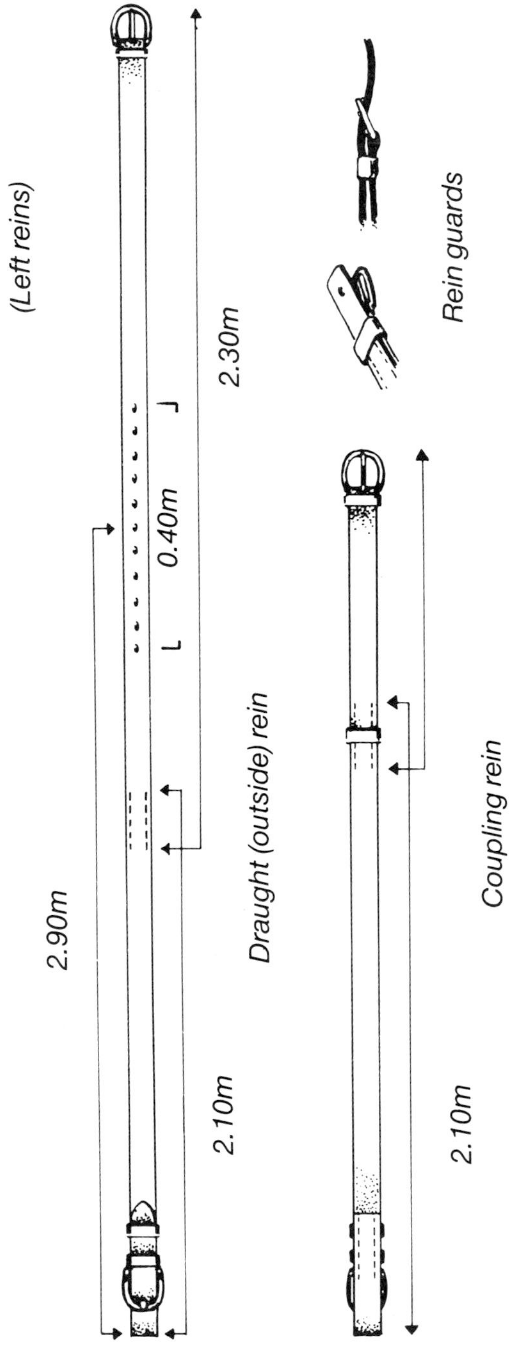

(Left reins)

2.30m

2.90m

0.40m

Draught (outside) rein

2.10m

Rein guards

Coupling rein

2.10m

designs, for example 'German crossed reins', and fulfil all the necessary requirements.

Achenbach reins
The essential characteristics of the Achenbach reins are:

☐ The use of reins of a specified length, combined with the use of a fixed splinter bar – possibly with individual swingle trees, but without an 'evener' (see Section 3.3) – and a particular driving technique, which permits optimum action on all of the horses.

☐ Eleven holes on the draught (outside) rein, which are oval to facilitate quick adjustment of the coupling reins. The holes are spread over a length of 40cm and are equidistant, i.e. 4cm apart. The distance from the holes to the driver's hand is such that they can be adjusted from the box even during the drive to obtain equal distribution of the work, but they must not be so close that they get in his way.

☐ A single oval hole on the rein billet and a long, and therefore easy-to-operate, buckle. There is only one hole on the billet, so that the adjustment has to be made at the coupling.

☐ A keeper, sewn to the inside (coupling) rein, which holds both reins together.

☐ Buckle guards underneath the coupling buckles to prevent the reins becoming brittle at this point and to avoid the formation of ugly black marks on the reins.

☐ The buckle on the inside (coupling) rein is sewn on 'upside down'. On all other parts of the harness the smooth side of the leather (grain side) is uppermost, but on coupling reins the 'flesh side' is uppermost. If the coupling buckle were sewn on the 'right way round', on crossed reins the inside (coupling) rein would always be twisted. Sewing the buckle in this way allows the rein to lie correctly.

Viennese or Hungarian reins
In spite of the provision of more coupling holes, it is impossible with Viennese (Hungarian) reins to com-

pensate for different temperaments and to distribute the work load with the same precision as with the Achenbach reins. Many whips see as the main advantage of the Viennese (Hungarian) pair reins the fact that each horse can be driven with a separate rein (because the driver has four reins in his hand, and not two as with the Achenbach pair reins).

The essential characteristics of the Viennese (Hungarian) reins are:

☐ Four holes on the rein billets.

☐ The inside rein runs through a metal (or ivory) ring sewn on to the outside rein.

☐ The couplings are in the driver's hand and are known as the 'frog'.

☐ On each of the four reins there are up to twenty buckle holes – i.e. up to eighty in all.

2(6) Additional and Auxiliary Equipment

Mentioned below are a few items sometimes used with single turnouts and pairs. Although they do not constitute part of the necessary equipment, and some are not at present permitted in driving competitions, they can be of use occasionally in the training of harness horses or in everyday driving.

Bearing reins are only occasionally to be recommended for use in the schooling of horses with poor conformation, and then only in the hands of experts. The bearing reins are hooked on to the bearing hook of the saddle or pad by means of a loop sewn at the end of them. They then pass through the bridoon hangers on either side of the headpiece and run down each side of the horse's head and are attached to the bit or, better still, to a bridoon used in addition to the horse's normal bit.

Bandages protect the horse's cannon bones from external injury.

44

Bucephalus noseband is sometimes used with success on horses who offer excessive resistance to the action of the bit. The hooks at the end of the noseband are attached to the curb hooks, if a curb is used, or to the floating ring, if a Wilson snaffle is used.

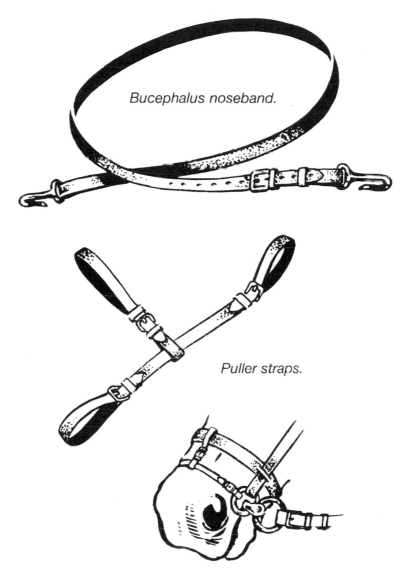

Bucephalus noseband.

Puller straps.

Curb guard made of leather or rubber, protects thin-skinned horses from sores caused by the rubbing or pressure of the curb chain.

Puller straps* are used with horses who are heavy in hand to transfer part of the action of the bit on to the bottom of the nasal bone and thus teach them not to pull. Puller straps are only permissible for exercise and training.

Sallengs are artistically braided leather straps with long fringes, used with Hungarian harness primarily for decoration and only to a lesser extent as fly guards.

Brushes/burrs are fitted on the shaft or pole to stop the horse from constantly leaning on it. They should be used with the utmost care since horses are inclined to react to them by kicking.

Brushing boots protect the horse's fetlocks from injuries. It is wise to carry a set, particularly on long journeys, because horses are prone to injure themselves by brushing (striking the foot against the opposite fetlock) when they are tired or if a shoe needs replacing.

Cruppers, heavily padded and sometimes with a support projecting to the rear, are used to improve the tail carriage of horses who keep their tails clamped down, and to prevent the reins being trapped under their tails.

* Puller straps have the same effect as a Kineton noseband on a ridden horse.

3. The Vehicle

3(1) Types of Vehicle

The vehicles in use today can be classified under the following headings: *phaeton*, *dog cart*, *gig*, *'jagdwagen'* (*hunting phaeton*, *Beaufort phaeton*) and *brake*. There are numerous different types of vehicle, some with the most imaginative names, but they can all be traced back to these basic types.

The essential criteria for any type of vehicle are:

☐ Stability.
☐ Lightness.
☐ Manoeuvrability.
☐ Safety.

As well as fulfilling these requirements the vehicle must also suit the purpose for which it is intended and it must be used with the correct form of turnout – for example the phaeton is a pair vehicle, the dog cart is for a single, and the brake is definitely a team vehicle.

Nowadays good vehicles are produced to order by a few specialised firms. Unfortunately there are a lot of impractical and unattractive vehicles on the market. For ponies, in particular, it is difficult to find really serviceable vehicles.

For competitions, especially international ones, set weights and widths are laid down for the vehicle in each phase. Details are set out in the Fédération Equestre Internationale rules and also, in Britain, in the *Horse Driving Trials National Rules*. With today's mass production methods and machine-made parts, there is little opportunity for the driver to have any say in the manufacture of the vehicle. Nevertheless, a basic knowledge of vehicle construction and the design of the different parts is of some interest to the educated whip.

Dog cart.

Jagdwagen (hunting/Beaufort phaeton).

Stanhope phaeton.

Coach or drag.

Char-à-banc.

Spider phaeton.

3(2) The Wheels

Carriage wheels consist of a hub, spokes and a rim (with a tyre). The tyre may be solid rubber, pneumatic or iron. The construction of the wheels has considerable effect on the utilisation of the pulling power. The larger the wheel, the more freely the vehicle runs. Small wheels cause a good deal of resistance, particularly on bumpy tracks and across country.

Large wheels often make it difficult for the whip and passengers to get in and out of the vehicle, and can sometimes have an adverse effect on the vehicle's ability to turn. If they are used, there must be room for them to turn underneath the body of the vehicle. As a compromise, on some vehicles the front wheels are small and the back wheels large. However, since small front wheels affect the angle of draught (from the collar to the splinter bar), this solution is not to be recommended.

Nowadays, the wheel hub usually contains either a grease- or oil-filled patent plain bearing or ball bearing. The hubs are attached to the axle and, because of the friction caused by the wheel turning, they need to be checked carefully to make sure that there is plenty of grease or oil in them.

In order to place as little strain as possible on the wheel nuts when the wheel is moving, and to direct the centrifugal force inwards to the middle of the axle, the axle arms slope downwards slightly.

To ensure that the oblique setting of the wheels does not cause the tyres to come in contact with the ground on the outside only, the spokes are attached to the hub at a slight angle, and point outwards: the wheels are said to be 'dished'. Dishing the wheels also has the advantage that dirt thrown up by the wheel during the journey is flung outwards. Pneumatic tyres, as used on motor vehicles, have given good results on various types of vehicle, especially those used regularly in traffic. Wooden spoked wheels are usually protected by a solid rubber or iron tyre.

The front wheels should have the same track width as the rear ones. A wide track increases the stability of the vehicle. For competition driving (driving trials), a minimum width of 1.60m is laid down.*

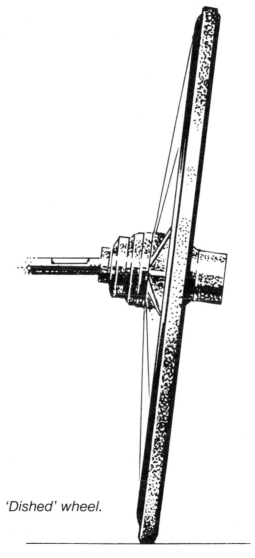

'Dished' wheel.

* This measurement applies to horse teams for the obstacle driving phase only. For other minimum measurements, see FEI rules and British *Horse Driving Trials National Rules*.

3(3) Vehicle Bodies, Springs and the Driver's Seat

The body of the vehicle provides the facility for carrying the whip, the passengers and, possibly, goods. The classification of carriages is based on whether or not they are enclosed, the number of people they are designed to carry and the space available for carrying goods.

The body of the vehicle is usually connected to the axle, and thus to the wheels, by steel springs. Unsprung vehicles, which have a direct, rigid connection with the axle – for example, vehicles with a perch undercarriage – are sometimes used in agricultural or tradesman's turnouts.

On a four-wheeled vehicle the body is connected to the front axle by the fifth wheel, or turntable. It is this which makes it possible for the front wheels to turn. The turntable is one of the parts of the carriage which require regular maintenance. Unless it is clean and well greased, the vehicle will be difficult to turn, which will result in excessive wear and tear on the horses. The connection between the front wheels and the turntable, and the body and the turntable, must also be checked regularly to make sure that the vehicle is roadworthy.

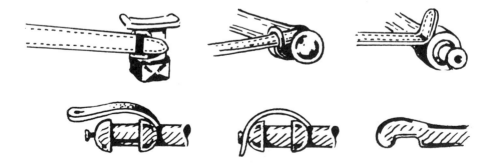

Methods of attaching the traces to the swingle tree.
Translator's note: In Great Britain, hooks on the swingle tree/splinter bar are the commonest form of attachment with single harness.

Attached rigidly to the front axle, the front springs and the turntable is the splinter bar, to which the horses' traces are attached. There are three different types of attachment:

☐ To swingle trees attached to the splinter bar (the most rational way for the educated whip).

☐ To fixed 'roller bolts' on the splinter bar (only possible with full collar harness; if used with a breastcollar, the horse's chest would be rubbed).

☐ To swingle trees attached to a moveable bar or 'evener'. This method is used with agricultural vehicles, for ploughing and for heavy draught.*

The springs, which connect the body to the axle of the vehicle, are designed either so that the body rests on top of them – thus they actually carry the body – or so that the body is slung between them. They may consist of a number of metal leaves in two sections, top and bottom (elliptic springs), or they may be of the type which are not fixed down at one end (Cee springs). Depending on the design of the vehicle, the springs may run lengthways down the sides of the vehicle (side springs) or across it (cross springs). With cross springs, swinging of the body from side to side is inevitable, especially when driving across country.

The body contains the seats for the whip and passengers. For safety, correct height and construction of the driver's seat are essential. The driver's seat is on the front right-hand side of the body, which enables him to use the brake and to observe the traffic. For correct control of the horses, the driver must sit higher than the croup of the horse in front of him. The best type of seat, especially for a team vehicle, is one with a wedge-shaped cushion which is higher at the back than at the front. The height should be such that the whip can sit with his knees slightly bent, his feet on the slightly sloping floor

* The evener works like a see-saw on its side: it equalises the draught, but the horses are not at a constant distance from the driver's hand, making accurate rein-handling virtually impossible.

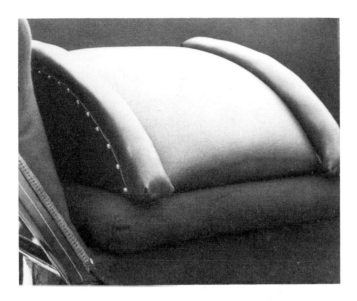

Seat cushion particularly suited to team driving, providing the driver with a firm, raised seat and so giving him more control.

Left: Fixed splinter bar with swingle trees. The 'roller bolts' are clearly visible on the splinter bar.

of the vehicle (*footboard*), and the whole area of his seat in contact with the cushion. He must be able to tighten the muscles in the small of his back at any time in order to hold a horse who leans on the bit.

The part of the vehicle body which is in front of the whip's legs is the *dashboard*. It serves to protect the whip and passengers from mud thrown up during the journey, and at the same time gives some protection against falling out of the vehicle.

3(4) Shafts and Pole

The *shafts* are two slightly bent wooden or metal poles attached to the splinter bar on the front of the vehicle. In a single turnout the horse is placed between these shafts. The shafts must be far enough apart for the horse to have

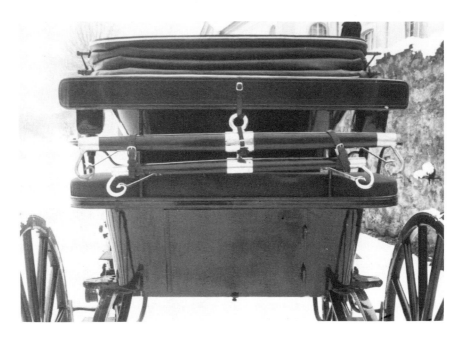

A good method of attaching the spares to the vehicle: main bar and lead bar.

complete freedom of movement. Their length should be such that when the horse is *in draught* (that is, when the traces are taut) the tip of the shaft is level with the point of the horse's shoulder, that is, level with his chest. They must never be too short, otherwise there is a risk that they will dig into the horse's body behind his shoulder or elbow when pulling up, causing serious injury.

On the front third of the shafts are sideways projecting, hooked-shaped attachments (*tug-stops*) for the tugs to rest against. Screws with large, protruding heads are unsatisfactory for this purpose because they are not safe. Since they often take all the strain when the horse is pulling up or holding the vehicle back, for maximum safety they must be made of the best materials.

A 'D' is screwed on to the rear third of the shaft to take

the kicking strap, with the 'D' for the breeching slightly in front of it. Depending on the type of vehicle, there may be a *swingle tree* at the base of the shafts. The swingle tree serves as the point of attachment for the shafts, and is movable. The shafts may be attached permanently to the splinter bar or they may be removable, depending on the design of the vehicle.

On the splinter bar are the *roller bolts*, to which the traces may be attached if full collar harness is used. The heads of the roller bolts are 5 to 8cm in diameter and the bolts are situated on the left and right ends of the splinter bar, as close to the ends as possible.

A *pole* is used where two horses are harnessed abreast. It serves to steer the vehicle, to stop it (braking) and, where applicable, to attach the equipment required for additional horses (*main bar* and *lead bars* for a four-in-hand, *swing pole* for a six-in-hand). The pole should be made of a pliable type of wood – ash is suitable – and should be constructed from a single piece of wood. The pole length for a vehicle drawn by full-sized horses is 2.80m, measured from the swingle trees to the pole head. (It actually extends beyond the swingle trees to allow for attaching it to the vehicle.) The end of the pole should not protrude beyond the horses' foreheads when they are stood up in their traces (when the traces are taut). Short poles are dangerous because when the horses are in heavy draught the end is back behind the horses' elbows, where it can cause serious injury. The pole is attached to the vehicle by putting it between two metal eyes on the turntable underneath the splinter bar, and securing it with a pin (*pole pin*).

With normal-sized horses the end of the pole should be about 1 to 1.05m above the ground, and it should not be carried by the horses' necks. With ponies, or very large horses, the point of the shoulder can be used as a guide to the height of the pole. At the front end of the pole is the *pole head*, which bears the attachments for the pole straps. Because of the strain placed on it when holding

Pole head with crab, for teams.

the vehicle back (braking), the pole head must be made of best quality materials. The front section of the pole head must be able to turn to bring the pole strap rings into a vertical position so that if a horse falls, injury is avoided and the pole does not break. On vehicles with which pole *chains* are used (town turnout) the rings on the pole head are round, but where pole *straps* are used (for example, country turnout) they are oval. Pole heads on vehicles also used for team driving are equipped with a *crab* for the attachment of the main bar. It is important that there should be a strap across the gap between the end of the crab and the pole to prevent the wheelers getting their bits or harness caught on it.

3(5) Brakes

A brake is essential* to avoid unnecessary wear and tear on the horses. An educated driver uses the brake frequently and correctly. A bad driver lets the horses hold the vehicle back with the pole straps, or even allows it to run into the back of their hocks.

There are several different types of brakes:

☐ The spindle brake, operated by the driver's hand.

☐ The push-on brake, operated by the driver's hand.

☐ The pull-on brake (lever pull brake), operated by the driver's hand.

☐ The foot brake.

Drag shoes (*skid pans*) also deserve a mention, though they are only used occasionally, for example in mountainous areas.

The hand-operated brakes are located on the right-hand side of the vehicle, next to the driver's seat. The spindle brake, which works best in hilly areas, is operated either by a wheel (wind-on brake) or a crank. The push-on and pull-on brakes are operated by a lever and ratchet assembly positioned in reach of the driver's hand, directly beside his seat. The pull-on variety is definitely preferable, since the driver tends to move his body and left hand backwards when using it. When using a push-on brake the upper body leans forward, the left hand goes forward with it, and the horses actually increase their tempo while the brake is being applied.

The braking operation is usually brought about by wooden or hard rubber brake blocks acting on the tyre. Pneumatic-tyred vehicles have brake drums in the hubs, like motorbikes.

The foot brake pedal is on the footboard of the vehicle body and must be within easy reach of the whip's right or left foot. A disadvantage of foot brakes is that the driver can trip over the pedal when mounting or dismounting, or get the end of the reins caught on it.

* Refers to four-wheeled vehicles.

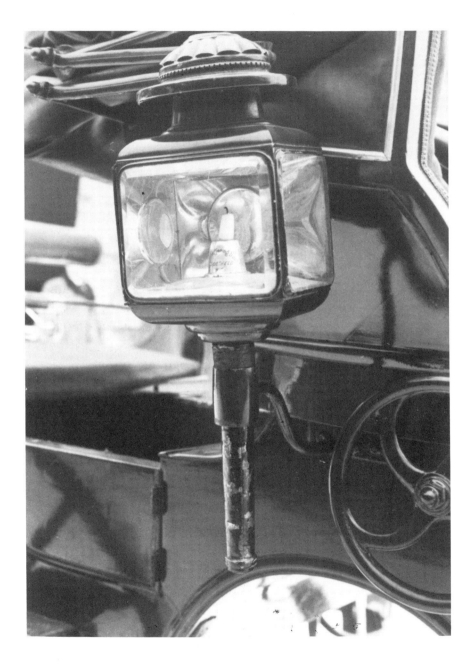

Regulation carriage lamps.

However, weighed against this is the fact that it is easy to use and leaves the hands free. Vehicles fitted with foot brakes should also have a hand brake.

All brakes should be as noise-free as possible when in operation. Brake blocks made of white beech, willow, poplar or lime wood are good because they do not make much noise.

The mechanical parts of the brakes must be kept well greased. The driver must ensure that any excess grease is wiped off immediately, so that he or his passengers do not get it on their clothes.

3(6) Lighting*

In common with all other vehicles which travel on the public high road, horse-drawn vehicles must be fitted with a functional lighting system. The legal requirement is at least one white (colourless) light showing to the front, and at least one red light showing to the rear. The bottom of the lamp glass must not be lower than 0.60m from the ground, and the top not higher than 1.55m.

The method of lighting – candle, battery or dynamo – is optional. For competitions it is good style to have a carriage lamp with a candle on either side of the vehicle at the front.

A further legal requirement is a red reflector, on the back of the vehicle, not more than 0.90m above the road. Both the lights and the reflectors at the rear should be as close as possible to the outside edges of the vehicle, and under no circumstances must a light be more than 0.40m from the widest point of the vehicle.

The driver is responsible for ensuring that the lighting equipment is clean, functional and not obscured (by passengers, blankets, etc.).

*Current British regulations can be found in the *British Driving Society Book of Driving*.

4. Care of Equipment and Carriage

Harness and good quality vehicles are expensive, and only last if they are regularly and correctly cleaned and maintained. Harness and vehicle should be cleaned every time they are used. As far as harness is concerned, a damp sponge or cloth is used to wipe off the dirt, and then saddle soap is applied to all the leather parts. Vehicles are best washed down with a hose pipe – wiping the dirt off tends to ruin the finish. The upholstery is brushed over. Metal parts, such as bits, and metal fittings on the carriage, are wiped with a damp cloth. At every cleaning session the stitching on the harness, the moving parts of the bit, and the vehicle are checked for damage.

To preserve the leather once it has been cleaned, it must be greased or oiled – the harness must, of course, be completely taken apart beforehand. Leather parts which do not come in direct contact with the horse should have a thin layer of special harness grease rubbed into them. (Patent leather must not come into contact with grease, but is cleaned with special patent-leather cleaner.) Leather parts which do come into contact with the horse, such as the inside of the collar or breastcollar and the saddle lining, are treated with tack oil (leather dressing) after cleaning.

Leather needs moisture if its firm, fibrous structure is to be conserved. The aim of greasing it is to keep the moisture in. Oil (the sort sold for maintaining leather) keeps the leather supple, but if used in excess it softens the fibres and causes the leather to lose its firmness.

A thin film of oil is smeared over the clips and buckles. Fittings on the harness, such as rosettes, may be cleaned and polished with metal polish. Chemical cleaners should not, however, be used on the mouthpieces of bits.

Stitching which has come undone must be repaired immediately. Metal fittings with cracks in them or sharp edges must be replaced at once. Harness should be stored in a dust-free, not-too-dry room, which is heated in winter. It must be hung on rounded wooden or metal hangers so that it does not crack or split. Wet leather should be dried out in the open air, never in blazing sunshine or in a hot oven.

When cleaning carriages, plenty of water should be used. Dirt must be removed before it has a chance to dry on. However, water must never be left lying in corners of the vehicle body, where it rots the wood. After washing, the carriage should therefore be gone over with a wash-leather and be well dried. Avoid washing a vehicle in the sun, since it damages the varnish or finish. Upholstery, floor coverings, etc, are brushed, vacuum cleaned and occasionally beaten.

The moving parts of the carriage, such as the wheels and the turntable, require special attention. Every time the vehicle is used, the turntable in particular should be greased or oiled before setting out.

After use, all the dirt must be removed before it dries on.

The wheel hubs must be greased at the point where they are joined to the axles. Every whip should learn how to grease the hubs. Since most vehicles nowadays have patent hubs and axles it is advisable to ask a specialist in carriage building or a mechanic how this should be done.

After every drive and during every cleaning session, the vehicle must be checked over for road-worthiness. Wheels should be examined for play and bolts, hubs and axles for tightness. The brakes and brake blocks must be in good condition and the lights in working order.

Vehicles should be stored in a clean, well-ventilated, dust-free building. If necessary, a cover should be put over them. The pole should be removed and hung up so that it does not become distorted. Pole straps or chains should also be removed after every drive and checked to make sure that they are safe.

Vehicles for singles need not have the shafts removed if they are put into storage for a short period. On four-wheeled vehicles the shafts should be raised and secured so that they cannot fall down. If the carriage is stored on a long-term basis, the shafts should be removed and hung up with the tips downwards. Before and after every drive the pins attaching the shafts to the carriage should be checked. Damage to the shafts must be repaired immediately, otherwise it may lead to a broken shaft and possibly a serious accident.

5. Teaching Driving: Instructional Aids

5(1) Construction and Use of the Driving Apparatus

The *driving apparatus* is used for teaching the pupil how to hold and handle the reins. It makes it possible to give a thorough training to several pupils at a time, and without upsetting the horses. To teach pupils the correct position of the hands and how to hold the whip, a small stick is used initially instead of a whip. Holding the reins correctly seems uncomfortable to start with. Just as a person learning to ride finds that his 'riding muscles' ache. The pains which he experiences in his hands and forearms must be overcome.

The driving apparatus can be made at home at little cost, and carried to the place where it is required. It is a good idea to construct it so that it can also be used later for teaching pupils to handle team reins. Two metal or plastic rollers of about 2 to 3cm in diameter are bolted or pinned into a 20cm-long piece of square-section hardwood, in which square holes have been made for the purpose. The rollers are fixed in such a way that they can turn. A piece of cord about 20cm long is threaded round each roller, and a weight or a bag filled with sand (about 1kg each) is attached to one end of each cord. An ordinary riding rein is attached to the other end. The block of wood with rollers in it is fixed to a wall or the edge of a table with a hook or other such attachment, which allows it to move about. A driving apparatus consists of two such blocks attached about 40 to 50cm apart. For practising handling pair reins, the lower pair of reins ('wheeler reins') is used.

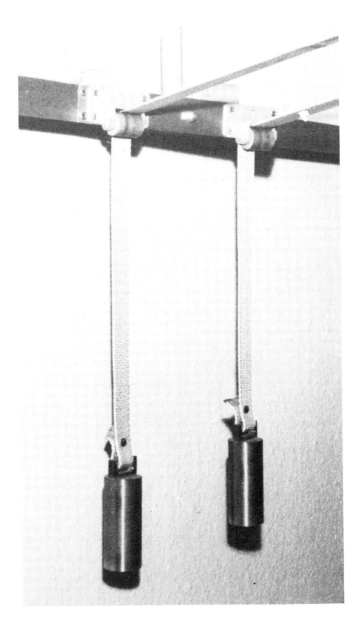

Driving apparatus.

5(2) Wooden Reins

Wooden reins are another aid which can be used for theoretical instruction. They teach the student how the Achenbach rein-coupling system works. The stiffness of the wood out of which they are made illustrates very clearly the principles of correct coupling. Wooden reins are made from thin strips of wood, approximately 2 x 1cm in cross-section, and are constructed according to the original measurements, but scaled down to half size. The coupling buckles are replaced by easily removable pegs.

5(3) Practice in Handling the Whip

For practice in using the whip and developing the accuracy of the aim, a *dummy horse* may be put in front of the carriage. This can consist of a board about 1.5m long, standing on two supports (jump stands or similar) about 1.30m off the ground and parallel to the pole (like a horse). The student practises touching a specified point with the lash of the whip. For practice in the use of a team whip, a 'leader' is added to the 'turnout'. It is important that the student always practises from the box, so that when he comes to do the real thing he does not find any difference.

5(4) Terminology

With pairs, the side nearest to the pole is the *inside*, and the other the *outside*, hence the descriptions *inside trace*, *outside trace*, and so on.

☐ On a left-hand turn the left horse is the *inside* horse; on a right-hand turn the right horse is the *inside horse*.

☐ The term *inside rein to the right (left)* horse is used *not* 'right (left) inside rein'.

☐ To *put the horse on the bit* means to establish a contact between the horse's mouth and the whip's hand.

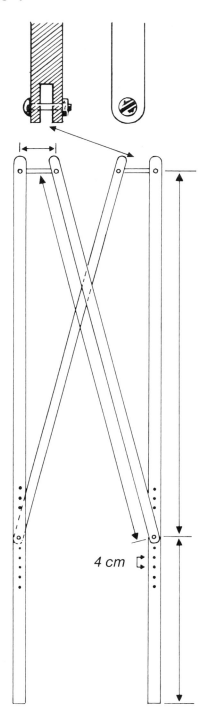

How to make 'wooden reins'.

68

☐ *Feeling the horse's mouth* (by squeezing the reins) consists of increasing the contact momentarily between the horse's mouth and the whip's hand, to cause the horse to take less of a hold on the bit and to pay more attention to the forthcoming command.

☐ *Collection* is the next stage on from being *on the bit*, and results from energetic engagement of the hind legs towards the centre of gravity.

☐ A horse is said to *fall apart* when he stretches out his neck so that he is no longer on the bit and trails along without impulsion.

☐ A horse is said to be *above the bit* when he carries his nose too high and evades the aids in an upward direction.

☐ A horse is said to be *behind the bit* when he overbends in his neck; and the line of his nose is permanently behind the vertical.

☐ A horse has a *hard mouth* when he does not mouth the bit (his mouth is 'dead'), when he leans on the bit and obeys only strong rein aids.

☐ A horse is well *in hand* when he obeys all the aids willingly and with a light contact with the whip's hand.

☐ The horse is *falling in on the turn* when he looks outwards with his head and drops his inside shoulder into the turn.

☐ The horses are said to be *hanging* or *leaning away from the pole* when they lean outwards against the outside trace and run the risk of losing their footing and slipping under the pole.

☐ The horses are said to be *leaning against the pole* when they lean their bodies against the pole or lean against each other above the pole.

☐ *Plain cheek, rough cheek, middle bar* and *bottom bar* refer to the part of the bit to which the rein is attached. Generally speaking, the lower down the cheek the rein is attached, the more severe the action.

6. The Basic Theory of the Achenbach System of Driving

6(1) The Correct Use of the Achenbach Reins

For Achenbach reins to be used correctly the measurements must be correct. These measurements are given in section 2(5), *Pair reins*. Only if they are correct will the full advantages of the system be gained.

If the horses are not working equally, the driver must decide how the couplings may be adjusted to remedy the situation. Getting the horses to work equally is only achieved by adjusting the couplings, and *never* by altering the traces. The horses should share the work equally and should be straight. The whip can tell when the horses are pulling equally – with a fixed splinter bar, of course★ – because the pole will be straight and equidistant between the two horses. If they are not doing the same amount of work, the pole will be at an angle, and will point towards the lazy horse.

If, when going straight ahead, the horses' heads both point outwards, the inside reins (coupling reins) are too long. If both horses' heads are permanently facing inwards, the inside reins are too short. However, the position of the reins should always be checked first – they may have been put through the wrong terrets. The continuous rein (draught rein) always stays on the outside: only the coupling reins should come inside.

If the horses are of normal height and more or less equal in temperament and build, both couplings should be done up on the sixth hole (counting from the whip's hand). This means that the inside reins are 12cm longer than the outside reins, which makes up for the longer

★ Not with eveners (see section 3.3).

70

distance they have to travel by crossing over. This setting is the normal or basic setting.

If the horses are very broad, the inside rein needs to be even longer, because the tops of the horses' backs, and so the two inside terrets on the pads, are further apart. To lengthen the inside reins, couple them on the seventh or even eighth holes (always counting from the whip's hand).

With narrow horses the inside reins will be too long, because the terrets are closer together, so in the basic setting the reins should be coupled on the fifth or fourth hole.

In the basic setting, which is used with horses of similar size, temperament and build, there is the same number of holes between the whip's hand and the buckle on each rein, hence:

☐ Basic setting for medium-sized horses (sixth hole) = 10 holes in all between hand and buckles.

☐ Basic setting for large, broad horses (seventh/eighth hole) = 12 to 14 holes between hand and buckles.

☐ Basic setting for small, narrow ponies (fourth/fifth hole) = 6 to 8 holes in all between hand and buckles.

In the case of ponies there is a risk that with Achenbach reins the buckles will be permanently in or even behind the whip's hand because they are coupled so far back. In such instances shorter reins should be used. However, it is important that when the couplings are on the normal setting (i.e. halfway down the line of holes) the inside reins are 12cm longer than the outside ones. If the horses have different temperaments, the coupling rein to the more forward-going horse is buckled further back than in the basic setting, and that of the less forward-going horse is lengthened accordingly, so that there is the same total number of holes between the hand and the buckle as in the basic setting.

The following is an example of how the couplings may be adjusted. The left horse of a pair is livelier, the right horse's traces are slacker than those of the left horse and

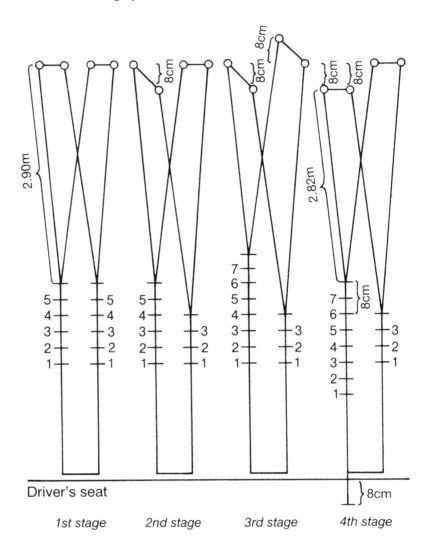

Driver's seat

1st stage   2nd stage   3rd stage   4th stage

The four stages in shortening the left horse's reins:
1st stage: Normal setting.
2nd stage: Shortening the right inside (coupling) rein by moving the buckle further back.
3rd stage: Lengthening the left inside rein by moving the buckle further forward.
4th stage: Shortening the left outside (draught) rein by moving it about 8cm further back through the hand.

72

the pole points permanently to the right. The solution is to shorten the inside (coupling) rein which goes to the left horse (attached to the right draught rein). The coupling rein to the right horse (attached to the left draught rein) is then lengthened by the same number of holes as the other has been shortened. This means that there are still 10 holes between hand and buckles, as in the basic setting. Since this adjustment causes the horses' heads to be at an angle (in this example they would be pointing to the right), the whip must shorten the appropriate rein (here, the left rein) through the hand by the same amount that he has shortened and lengthened the couplings.

The adjustment of the couplings is different if breast-collar harness is used. If the same basic setting is used with breastcollar harness as with full collar, the inside reins will be too long, because they do not pass through a terret on the collar but go direct from the pad to the bit. The coupling reins need to be shortened by about one hole. In other words, the basic setting for narrower horses should be adopted.

6(2) Holding the Reins: Single Harness and Pairs

The reins are held in the same way for singles and for pairs.

The basic rules are as follows:

☐ Both reins are always held in the left hand. The reins are divided by the index finger and middle finger of the left hand. The left rein lies on top of the index finger and the right rein lies under the middle finger (basic position).

☐ Both hands participate in handling the reins unless the right hand is required for some other purpose (using the brake or whip).

☐ A rein should never be allowed to slip through the fingers. The reins are shortened or lengthened only by the prescribed method.

☐ Only the horses are stopped by the reins (when a four-wheeled vehicle is used). The vehicle is stopped by the brake. If the brake is not used enough, the horses' mouths become hard and insensitive.

☐ All turns are performed by yielding the outside rein, not by pulling the inside rein.

☐ Whip aids are always given by the right hand, which is taken off the reins beforehand so as not to disturb the horses' mouths.

☐ The brake is operated by the right hand. The whip is transferred to the left hand beforehand, so that it does not touch the horses accidentally.

☐ If, owing to unforeseen circumstances, a dangerous situation suddenly arises, any suitable method of handling the reins may be adopted with a view to preventing an accident.

☐ The reins are secured by the lower three fingers of the hand. The thumb and forefinger must always be available to take the whip if necessary.

☐ Pulling and jerking the reins, which tends to be the layman's method of sending the horses forward, must be avoided. No one who fails to relinquish this habit will make a good whip.

There are three different positions for holding the reins:

☐ Basic position.

☐ Working position.

☐ Schooling (dressage) position.

The basic position forms the basis for driving singles and pairs. It also serves as a foundation for the position used for four-in-hands and six-in-hands.

The two reins lie flat, grain-side up, in the left hand, with the left rein on top of the index finger and the right between the middle and third fingers. Only the lower three fingers grip the reins as they come through the hand. The thumb and index finger of the left hand remain open and slightly bent, ready to take the whip at any time.

74

Holding the reins: basic position for pair driving.

Basic position.

The left hand is positioned about a hand's breadth in front of the middle of the abdomen, with the elbow lying without stiffness against the body. The knuckles are vertical and the hand is bent slightly inwards at the wrist.

The right hand holds the whip and is positioned half in front and half to the right of the left hand, and at the same height. About 10cm of the hand part of the whip protrudes below the hand, and the stick points forwards/upwards to the left.

Driving with the reins in the basic position must become second nature, so that the whip will experience no difficulties later on when he comes to drive teams.

The working position takes some of the strain off the left hand on long journeys. In the working position the left hand is the same as in the basic position. The right hand is placed on top of the right rein in front of the left

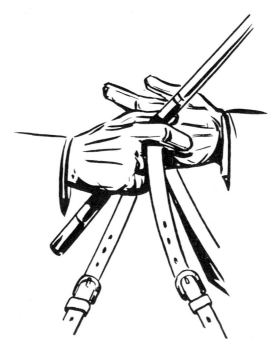

Working position (position for everyday driving).

hand, so that the right index finger is hooked over the left rein and the three lower fingers over the right rein, with the fingertips in contact with the flesh (underneath) side of the reins. The whip is held by the thumb and index finger of the right hand. If the hand position is correct, the whip, held at its point of balance (usually marked by a metal ring), goes into the correct position of its own accord, i.e. it points obliquely partly forwards, partly upwards and partly to the left.

As with the other positions, in the working position the left hand (which is still in the basic position) keeps a firm hold of the reins – a rein must never be allowed to slip. On long journeys the fingers of the left hand may be opened and moved a little to prevent them becoming tired, but in this case the fingers of the right hand must grip the reins especially tightly. However, even when this is being done, the fingers of the left hand should still remain in their position between the two reins.

The schooling position (dressage position). The left hand remains in the basic position as before. The right hand is placed over the right rein in the working position. The bottom three fingers (middle finger, fourth finger and little finger) hook around the right rein, and the hand is placed in a vertical position beside the left hand and about 10cm (maximum 15cm) to the right of it.

In order to adopt a vertical position, the right hand must pull a short length of rein through the left hand, but the left hand must not release the left rein while this is being done. The length of rein between the two hands is called the *bridging piece*. The driver must be able to change from the dressage position into the working position and the basic position quickly, and without altering the direction in which he is travelling, or the tempo, and without looking at his hands. Changing from one position to another must be practised thoroughly on the *driving apparatus*. Mistakes resulting in alterations in the length of the reins (which if made from the box will cause a change of direction) show up straight away on the *driving apparatus*. Only through constant practice will the student of driving acquire the necessary dexterity.

Schooling (dressage) position.

Gradual restraining action.

The dressage position is used for schooling; when the horses are not going straight; on bad roads; in difficult terrain, or in dressage tests where there is no particular requirement for another position.

The driver must always remember that whip aids can only be given from the basic position.

The position of the whip (pointing left, forwards and upwards) remains the same in the working position and the dressage position as in the basic position.

6(3) Taking up the Reins (Singles and Pairs), Mounting and Dismounting

To have proper control of the horses while mounting and sitting down, and to be able to move off straight away with impatient horses and so avoid an accident, it is essential to have the reins at the right length and in the basic position in the hand.

The reins are taken up as follows:

The whip stands on the left of the horses, level with and facing the pad or saddle, and about a stride away from the horses, so that he can reach them with his arm outstretched. With his right hand he takes both reins out from under the point strap (or backband on a single turnout) and lays the hand parts over his left forearm. This prevents the ends of the reins being dropped on the ground and becoming dirty.*

The right hand takes hold of the right rein (grain side up) just behind the coupling buckle (with single reins just behind the splice). The rein passes between the index finger and the middle finger and runs down through the hand. The hand establishes a light contact with the horses' mouths. The whip then checks that the reins are not caught on anything. Keeping the contact with the horses' mouths, the right hand slides down the right rein

* In Britain it is traditional for the driver to mount from the right, i.e. on the same side that he sits, though it is often more practical to mount from the left so as to avoid standing in the path of the traffic.

until the arm is hanging down by the right side, where it must remain. The left hand takes the left rein and transfers it to the right hand so that it runs down through the whole hand. The left hand then lengthens the left rein by pulling it through the hand until the left coupling buckle is 5cm further out than the right. Since the whip sits on the right-hand side of the vehicle, the left rein has further to go and must therefore be approximately this much longer. However, this measurement applies to pairs of normal-sized horses. With singles the whip may sit directly behind the horse, in which case the rein is not lengthened at all.

Both reins are then transferred to the left hand in the basic position (index and middle fingers between the reins). Finally the whip lengthens the reins, with his right hand in the working position, by the amount required for him to reach the box. (The reins must not, however, be allowed to slide through the hands.) The use of this procedure ensures that the whip has an even contact with the horses' mouths immediately he sits down on the box. The amount by which the reins need to be lengthened to reach the box is usually about 20cm, though it depends on the distance of the box from the horses.

The reins can easily slip off the driver's forearm as he mounts, so it is a good idea to slip the little finger of the left hand through a small loop sewn on to the buckle end of the reins. This will prevent him putting his foot through the reins.

To prevent the horses stepping sideways, when the whip has lengthened both reins he should make a big loop with the left rein and hold it under his thumb. He then releases it as he mounts. Lengthening the left rein to allow for the whip sitting on the right of the vehicle means that if the horses move off prematurely, they will turn to the right (the side of the shorter rein). The loop in the left rein will prevent this; if the horses do move off prematurely, they will do so to the left, i.e. around the driver.

To mount, the whip walks back to the left front axle of the vehicle, without taking his eyes off the horses, and climbs up via the wheel hub and the step, holding on to the vehicle with his left hand. Once on the vehicle, with his right hand he picks up the whip, which is lying along the seat and sits down on the right. The loop in the left rein has been let out as he mounted, so that the reins are now even. The right hand is used to put the free end of the reins down beside the left thigh.

The reverse procedure is adopted for dismounting. The driver transfers the whip to the left hand, which holds the reins in the basic position, uses his right hand to lay the ends of the reins over his left forearm, stands up, and lays the whip across the seat. He then dismounts backwards, without taking his eyes off the horses. Once down, he gathers the reins up and puts them under the point strap (or back band), with the ends to the rear.

6(4) Shortening and Lengthening the Reins, Turning and Reining Back

Shortening and lengthening the reins is always performed by the right hand, with the hands in the working position. Letting the reins slip through the fingers is a very serious fault.

The holds used must be thoroughly practised on the driving apparatus. The whip must be able to shorten and lengthen the reins both individually and together with complete confidence, without looking down at them and with his attention still focused on the horses. The better he masters the handling of the reins with singles and pairs, the easier he will find it with teams of four or more.

Shortening both reins:
There are various ways of shortening the reins:

Both reins

By a few centimetres. Both reins may be shortened whenever required by placing the right hand in front of the left and using it to push the reins a few centimetres through the half-open left hand. The right hand must never be placed so far forward that the sections of rein between the two hands fold or twist, or the reins slip out of the left hand.

By a short length (gradual half-halt, gradual restraining action) e.g. before a right-hand turn. The hands start off in the working position. The left hand is then placed directly in front of the right, the right hand further forward still in front of the left in the working position, and finally the reverse procedure is adopted and the hands return to their original positions on the reins. This is the only exercise in which the left hand is taken off the reins, and is only possible with single turnouts and pairs.

Temporarily, by a lot (temporary restraining action) e.g. for pulling up (halting). From the working position the right hand transfers the whip to the left, applies the brake and then takes back the whip. It then moves the required distance (about 20cm) down the reins in the working position and closes on them. The reins are then brought back by the right hand while the left hand moves upwards out of the way. When the halt has been completed both hands return to their original position.

Shortening the reins by a lot (prolonged restraining action). If the reins have to be shortened for a longer period of time (e.g. to go down a hill, the right hand transfers the whip to the left and applies the brake. It then takes back the whip and takes hold of both reins behind and below the left hand with the lower three fingers so that they run down through the middle of the hand. The reins are then pulled through the left hand, which slides forward. The right hand moves in the direction of the right hip to give it room to take back the required amount of rein. When the necessary adjustment has been made, the right hand returns to the working position in front of the left hand, as soon as the latter is holding the reins securely again.

Lengthening both reins

There is only one way to lengthen both reins. The left hand remains in the basic position. From the working position, the right hand draws both reins slowly forward (not upward) and by the same amount through the left hand until the required length is reached, and then returns to the working position just in front of the left hand.

Lengthening and shortening individual reins

Lengthening and shortening individual reins requires dexterity, which can only be achieved by constant practice. The whip must remain steady in its correct forward/upward position throughout, and the thong must not touch the horses.

Lengthening the right rein. The right hand is in the working position. The index finger of the right hand grips the left rein a little more firmly. The right hand makes a twisting movement, in which the back of the hand turns to face upwards, and pulls the right rein out through the left hand with the three lower fingers. This movement may be repeated several times, as necessary.

Shortening the right rein. To shorten the right rein the whip makes the opposite movement to that used for lengthening it, i.e. he turns his hand in a clockwise direction and pushes the rein through the slightly open left hand. In this exercise, particular care must be taken not to catch the horses with the thong of the whip.

Lengthening the left rein. The right hand is in the working position, with the lower three fingers holding the right rein still. The hand turns clockwise around the

83

little finger, which acts as a pivot, and the right index finger pulls the left rein out through the left hand by a few centimetres. The movement is repeated as often as is necessary.

Shortening the left rein. Here the right hand makes the opposite movement to that used for lengthening the rein, i.e. anti-clockwise, and pushes the left rein in through the left hand. It is particularly difficult to keep the whip still during these exercises, which is why a stick should always be carried when practising on the driving apparatus.

NB *These instructions apply to carriages being driven on the right-hand side of the road, though see the third paragraph below.*

Turns
Basic observations:
☐ Most turns are made by yielding the outside rein and never by pulling the inside rein. This enables the outside horse to move freely forward and to pull the vehicle around. For this to work correctly, the vehicle must have a fixed splinter bar (see section 3.3).
☐ The horses must always be bent in the direction of the movement, i.e. their heads must not be turned outwards. This happens when horses become accustomed to turning at a certain point and do so of their own accord, throwing themselves into the turn without waiting for the aids to do so. The inside rein is used to give the horses the correct bend.
☐ The whip sits on the right-hand side of the vehicle so that he can use the brake, and to leave space for a passenger. Consequently he is not sitting over the centre axis of the vehicle but to the right of it, which explains the difference in the methods used for left- and right-hand turns.
☐ Right-hand turns on roads in Germany are always performed at a walk, but left-hand turns may be performed at a slow, collected trot, because they follow a

wider arc. The whip feels the horses' mouths before each turn to make them pay attention.

☐ If it becomes necessary to use the whip during the turn, it should be used only on the inside horse. If it is used on the outside horse, the latter will pull the vehicle too far into the bend. Moreover, it will cause the horses' heads to face outwards.

The left turn

The driver feels the reins, or in rare cases performs almost a full halt ('temporary restraining action') to decrease the tempo and to make the horses pay attention. When driving in traffic, or in a competition designed to find the best driver, the driver looks around to make sure that it is safe to cross the road and turn left. At the same time he gives the signal for turning left by raising his right arm above his head with the whip pointing left.

For turning, the driver takes the reins in the schooling position (dressage position). The backs of the hands turn upwards: first the right hand (this causes the right rein to yield and starts the horses turning), then the left (which indicates the direction and amount of bend in the horses' necks). When the back of the left hand turns upwards, the left rein should move behind the knuckles and run over the back of the hand. During the turn, both hands move towards the horses to allow them to move through the wide arc required in the left turn. If necessary, the right hand is taken off the rein to allow the left hand to yield sufficiently.

Only in the case of very large vehicles is it sometimes necessary for the whip to lengthen the reins slightly before the turn, using the method described earlier. With small or medium-sized vehicles, and particularly with single turnouts, it is usually sufficient to put the hands forward to lengthen the reins by the required amount but without losing the contact.

To go straight ahead again the left hand returns to the upright position (which causes the left rein to yield), then the right hand also resumes its former position, so that both hands are in the schooling position again.

The tempo can be increased again by yielding both reins before the turn is completed – in fact about half way through it.

If the left (inside) horse comes out of draught during the turn (which can be seen from the traces), it means that the whip has held the left rein too tightly or pulled it backwards. If the reins have been lengthened prior to a left-hand turn, they must be shortened again when the turn is completed. Since on the Continent the traffic drives on the right, left-hand turns are wide turns.

About-turn to the left ('U' turn)
On the Continent this is used for making 'U' turns on narrow roads. First the horses are brought back to a walk. Then the whip gives the appropriate traffic signal for a left turn (see above), the most important part of which is the looking to make sure that it is safe to turn. Before the actual turn the horses are brought back almost to a halt.

From the working position, the right hand lengthens the right rein by the amount necessary for the turn. The left hand turns so that the back of the hand is uppermost. It is essential that the rein runs across the back of the hand and not just across the knuckles. To go straight ahead again, the left hand resumes its upright position. The right hand moves down the right rein, takes hold of it, takes it out from the left hand, and replaces it further back to shorten it.

If the reins have to be lengthened during the actual turn, this is achieved by moving the left hand forward in the direction of the turn, towards the horses' mouths, with the reins in the basic position in the left hand. The right hand is ready to intervene if necessary and to lengthen the right rein only.

The right turn
The right turn is a tight turn, and is therefore driven

only at a walk. The driver slows down to a walk, using the one-hand-in-front-of-the-other method (as in a 'gradual half-halt') to shorten the reins. He then indicates that he intends to turn right by extending his arm to the right. The whip is transferred to the left hand while this is done.

When the right hand has taken back the whip it is moved about 10cm down the right rein and holds it firmly at this point. The left hand turns anti-clockwise (back of the hand downwards), which causes the left rein to yield. Only by turning inwards from the wrist can the right hand shorten the rein sufficiently for the turn and to obtain the necessary lateral flexion.

After the turn, both hands return to an upright position. The right hand slides back 10cm up the right rein and adopts the working position. Both reins are lengthened by the amount they were previously shortened, and the normal tempo is resumed.

Right about-turn ('U' turn).

Right 'U' turns are forbidden on the Continent, where the traffic drives on the right, because they create an obstruction and a danger to other road users. They are used in schooling horses to increase their dexterity, and as a test of the driver's skill, but are performed only on schooling grounds and in competitions.

The right hand makes the appropriate traffic signal to forewarn any drivers, pedestrians or riders who may be following. For the actual turn the horses are brought back almost to a halt by the 'gradual half-halt' method (shortening the reins by putting one hand in front of the other). As in the previous exercise, the right hand moves down the right rein, but this time it carries it back and then replaces it in the left hand about 10cm shorter. While the left hand, in the basic position, starts the horses on the turn by turning anti-clockwise (back of the hand downwards), the right hand again takes hold of the right rein in front of the left hand and asks for the correct flexion.

After the turn, the right hand returns to an upright position, lengthens the right rein by the amount it was shortened, and then lengthens both reins back to their original length. Finally, the working position is adopted and the turnout continues straight ahead.

Driving turns with one hand

Although the left hand is used on its own only when the right is occupied with the brake, whip, etc, a skilful driver should be in a position to obtain changes of tempo and direction using the basic position, i.e. one hand only. A slightly more positive contact with the horses' mouths is necessary.

Left-hand turns (one-handed) with singles or pairs are performed by turning the left hand clockwise (back of the hand uppermost), with the left rein running right over the back of the hand and not just over the knuckles. Turning the hand lengthens the right rein. If this is not sufficient in sharper turns, the left hand may be carried over towards the right hip.

Right-hand turns (one-handed). For these the reins may need to be shortened, but this can be done at the same time that the horses are brought back to a walk. To turn right, the left hand, which is in the basic position, turns

Rein running across the back of the hand.

anti-clockwise (back of the hand facing downwards), which lengthens the left rein and shortens the right. If this is not sufficient, the left hand may be carried over to the left hip. To conclude the turn, the hand resumes its original position and hold.

When driving on the roads, these turns must obviously be preceded by the appropriate arm or whip signal, in the same way as the turns in the working and dressage positions.

When driving with one hand, it is especially important that the three lower fingers of the left hand grip the reins firmly. Slipping reins can ruin the turn completely and cause loss of control.

Rein-back

The most practical method of reining back is with the hands in the schooling position and the reins sufficiently shortened beforehand. If the schooling position is used, any crookedness can be corrected by turning the hands.

Before reining back, the whip must work out exactly where he intends to go. Whether he is backing into a gateway, into a road or along the straight, the angles must be calculated exactly. The horses are collected to prepare them for the rein-back. The increased impulsion is received by the hand and converted into a calm, two-time backward stepping movement by means of 'taking' rein aids. The rein-back is terminated by yielding the reins.

If the horses rush back, this means that the aids were too strong. With young horses it is a good idea to choose a slight slope for practising the rein-back, because the vehicle can be pushed back more easily.

Very obedient, supple, experienced horses will rein back without being driven on and collected beforehand. As a rein aid, the 'temporary restraining action' is sufficient (see *Shortening both reins*).

Most important of all, the aids should not be abrupt, but soft and deliberate. The use of the voice (the command 'Back') is a useful back-up.

7. Practical Driver Training

7(1) Harnessing Up and Unharnessing

Putting the various items of harness and equipment on the horse is called harnessing up. This operation usually takes place in the stable. Just before harnessing up, the horse must be brushed over – patches of dung-, straw- or sweat-encrusted hair, or dirt in any other form, can cause galls and wounds if part of the harness lies directly on top of them.

Harnessing Up
The harness is put on in the following order:
□ The collar or breastcollar is put on.
□ The saddle or pad is put on.
□ The crupper is put over the horse's tail.
□ The girth is fastened.
□ The bridle is put on.
□ The reins are drawn through the terrets and fastened to the bit.

Although it is sometimes rather a nuisance, it is a good idea to have the horses tied up while they are being harnessed because they stand better. Before harnessing up, the driver sorts out the various pieces of harness. With young or skittish horses, individual pieces are sometimes put on bare (stripped) – e.g. just the collar or breastcollar without the traces attached – but with older, more experienced horses it can be put together beforehand so that it is ready to use. The driver then places the saddle or pad on his left forearm and takes hold of the breastcollar by the sides, at the points where the neck strap is attached. He puts the breastcollar carefully over the horse's head, taking care not to knock the eyes (the headcollar is removed for this

Putting on a full collar.

Putting the tail through the crupper.

operation). The breastcollar is then turned round on the horse's neck, going with and not against the direction of the mane, and the saddle or pad is placed on the back just behind the withers.

Full collar harness is put on in the same way, except that the collar is held upside down (the wide part at the top) by the hame draught eyes. The collar is then turned the right way up again in the direction of the mane, on the narrowest part of the horse's neck (i.e. just behind the poll) and is slid down on to the shoulders before the saddle or pad is placed on the back. While the collar is being put on, the false martingale should be held in one hand along with the hame draught eye so that it does not get in the way.

With young or very nervous horses it is a good idea to remove the hames, put the collar carefully over the head, and then put the hames and other parts (traces, pad, etc) on one at a time.

If the collar or breastcollar is not already attached to the pad (on pairs harness), the next job is to attach the traces or hame tugs to the point strap.

The crupper is then fitted by taking hold of the tail just below the dock; lifting it up level with the dock and taking hold of the dock along with it; and then passing the two together through the dock of the crupper, which is held in the other hand. The crupper is pushed right up to the top of the dock of the tail, and any trapped hairs are freed and smoothed down. Even with experienced horses who are used to this operation, the driver must stand next to the horse's quarters and not directly behind his hind feet, in case he kicks.

Cruppers with detachable dock pieces are not a good idea since the tail hairs can become caught in the buckles and pulled out. Moreover, if the tail hairs become caught up, the horse tends to get upset and may panic. Once the crupper is on, the pad or saddle can be placed in its correct position just behind the withers, and the girth can be fastened. The false martingale attached to the collar can then be fastened to the girth. With single harness, the belly band is not done up until the shafts are in position. With double harness, the (false) belly band is done up loosely.

The bridle can be put on in the same way as a riding bridle, as is described in Book 1, *Principles of Riding*. However, because of the greater weight of a driving bridle, the following method may also be used. The driver stands on the left-hand side of the horse's head. Holding the bridle by the headpiece in his right hand, he lifts it up so that it is about level with the horse's forehead, taking care not to hit the horse in the eyes with the blinkers. Holding the bit across its full width with his left hand, he pushes it into the horse's mouth and at the same time lifts the bridle up with his right hand. Once the headpiece is lying in its correct position behind the horse's ears, the forelock can be straightened out underneath the browband and face drop – the forelock is not pulled out over the top of the browband as on a riding bridle.

The throatlatch is fastened loosely enough to allow the head to be raised and flexed. There must be room to slide at least the flat of the hand between the throatlatch and the throat. The throatlatch buckle, especially the outside one on each bridle on double harness, should be level with the cheekpiece buckle. The noseband should be fastened so that two fingers can just be inserted between it and the horse's nose. Nosebands which are too loose do not fulfil their object, which is to transfer some of the pressure from the bit to the nose. The height of the noseband is adjusted where it is attached to the cheekpiece, so that it neither presses on the corners of the mouth nor rubs against the cheek bones.

The blinkers are attached to the cheekpiece throughout their length, i.e. there should not be a slit separating the top part of the blinker from the cheekpiece. The blinkers point outwards slightly and are adjusted so that the eye lies level with the top third of the blinker, which has a slight outward bulge in it. It is important that the blinkers do not touch the eyes or eyelashes. For this reason, the winker stays, which are made of stiff leather, bend the blinkers outwards.

The bit should not pull the corners of the mouth upwards, nor should it hang down and rattle against the teeth, especially the tushes in stallions and geldings. With both snaffles and curbs, but especially the latter, particular attention must be paid to the width of the bit. On a curb bit, the part of the cheekpiece above the mouthpiece should be angled slightly outwards so as not to rub the horse's cheeks. The length of the curb hooks should be such that the curb chain lies exactly in the curb groove. The curb hooks are fitted with the opening at the back to prevent them becoming caught on the pole head or on the adjacent horse. The curb chain should be adjusted so that it is in contact with the chin groove when the cheeks of the bit form an angle of about 45° with the mouth.

Finally, the reins are put through the terrets. They must always lie flat, with the grain side uppermost. It is a good idea to put the rein with the buckle on the end on the left and the other on the right. This makes it easier to buckle and unbuckle the reins.* It also ensures that the reins are always used on the same side, which is important with coupled reins.

On single harness the rein passes through a terret on the saddle and another on the neck strap. The billet end fastens on to the bit in whichever position is necessary or desired. If a mild action is required, with a Wilson snaffle the rein is buckled to both rings together. If the rein is buckled to the outside ring only, the action is more severe. On the various types of curb bit the action becomes more severe the further down the cheek of the bit the rein is buckled, since this increases the lever action on the curb chain.

In the 'rough cheek' setting the rein is buckled around the cheek immediately below the mouthpiece. With pairs, on the outside of the bit the rein passes round both the back half of the ring and the cheek of the bit, but on the inside it passes only round the cheek, since otherwise the sideways pull of the rein would cause the front of the ring to dig into the side of the horse's nose.

With pairs similar rules are observed. The grain side of the leather is uppermost, the rein with the buckle at the end is put on the left and the one without the buckle on the right. The coupling reins always point inwards, so that in every case, the outside rein is the draught rein.

With breastcollar harness the inside (coupling) rein is not passed through the ring sometimes found on the

*Some drivers prefer to leave the reins unbuckled to avoid the risk of getting their foot caught in them.

95

inside of the neckstrap (and which should not be there). Correct breastcollar pair harness does not have this ring because it would cause the neckstrap to be pulled away from the neck by the adjacent horse's rein.

On full collar harness the inside terret can move up and down, and the rein *is* passed through it when the horses are harnessed up. However, since when the horses are 'put to' the inside rein crosses over to the opposite horse, it is attached temporarily to the throatlatch by passing the end through the throatlatch from back to front and then bringing it round and back through the keeper next to the buckle. The outside rein is attached to the bit immediately. The hand parts of the reins, which with a pair have not yet been buckled together, are fastened to the terret on the pad or to the point strap in such a way that they will not hang down, get caught and break.

The traces are laid across the back, underneath the crupper backstrap.

After harnessing up, a check is made to ensure that the harness fits properly.

☐ On breastcollar harness the lower edge of the breast-piece lies about two fingers' breadth above the point of the shoulder but not on the base of the neck (when the neck is in a normal position). In heavy draught the horse lowers his neck and if the breastcollar is fitted any higher, it restricts the breathing. If it is fitted lower, it restricts the movement of the shoulders and forelegs.

☐ On double harness the pole strap ring is slightly to the inside of the breastcollar. If it is on the outside, the harnesses are the wrong way round i.e. the left (near) set of harness is on the right (off) horse and vice versa.

☐ The neck strap lies on the horse's neck just in front of the withers, at the point where the neck joins the withers. From there it slopes downwards and slightly forwards to the point where it is attached to the breastpiece. It must never slope backwards, which would cause heavy press-ure and injury. The job of the neck strap is to support the breastpiece, and the length is adjusted accordingly. It is not the function of the neck strap to support the pole.

☐ The pad lies on the horse's back about 10cm behind the highest point of the withers, and the top part of it must not touch the horse's back. If there is not enough room between the leather or metal tree, the pad needs restuffing. As a temporary measure a piece of sponge or a special protective pad may be used underneath it.

☐ The girth serves to secure the pad or saddle around the horse's middle. Its correct position is about a hand's breadth behind the elbow. If it is too close to the elbow it will cause galling. On pairs' harness the buckles are on the outside of each harness.

☐ The belly band, or false belly band, on double harness serves to restrict the sideways movement of the traces, and can therefore be done up fairly loosely. On this, too, the buckles are on the outside. On single harness the top extension of the belly band, the back band, which is thicker than the belly band, serves to support the tugs. The belly band itself serves to keep the tugs close to the saddle.

☐ The crupper, which is attached to the 'D' ring at the back of the pad or saddle, prevents the latter from slipping forward. The top strap of the crupper backstrap should not protrude beyond the last keeper in case a rein gets caught under it. The crupper should be short enough to keep the saddle or pad in its correct position just behind the withers, but should not be tight (it should be easily pressed down on to the horse's back in the middle). The dockpiece is stitched on and should have no buckles.

☐ The kicking strap on single harness runs through a loop on the backstrap of the crupper, and when attached to the shafts it should run over the top of the sacrum (croup) and behind the point of the hip.

☐ If breeching is used, the breeching body lies about a hand's breadth below the point of the buttock. When the horse is standing up in his traces there should be room to place a fist on both sides underneath the breeching body below the points of the buttocks. The loinstrap should be attached to the breeching body in such a way that the latter is horizontal – if it slopes, it will rub the hind legs. Trace bearers must not break the line of draught.

☐ Full collars must be well stuffed and must have an anatomically correct fit, i.e. they should be pear-shaped not egg-shaped, to conform to the shape of the neck. The collar should have as large a bearing surface as possible and should leave both the point of the shoulder and the wind pipe free. It fits correctly if a finger can be run down either side between the collar and the horse's neck, and if a fist can be inserted at the bottom between the collar and the wind pipe. To obtain a correct fit, the collar can be made wider or narrower by the use of different-sized kidney links. If the collar is too long, a wedge-shaped pad will bring about some improvement. The stuffing must be thick enough to prevent in any circumstances the hame tugs from rubbing against the collar.

The point of the hame strap should always face the inside (on a single it should point to the off side) to make it easier to undo if the horses fall. The false martingale, which passes through the kidney link and round the collar, attaches to the girth and helps to keep the collar in position against the horse's breast. The line of draught, i.e. the straightness of the traces, must not be broken through having the hame tug buckle too high or too low.

The same rules apply for the fitting of the pad or saddle with full collar harness as with breastcollar.

Unharnessing
After the horses have been taken out of the vehicle they are unharnessed in the reverse order to harnessing up.

☐ The reins are unfastened and pulled out through the terrets.

☐ The bridle is removed and the headcollar put on (the horse may be tied up to facilitate the rest of the operation).

98

☐ The girth is undone.

☐ The crupper is removed.

☐ The pad or saddle is removed and placed on the left forearm.

☐ The collar or breastcollar is removed. The horse is first untied, then the collar or breastcollar is turned over at the thinnest part of the horse's neck, grasped on both sides and carefully slid over the head. With sensitive horses the hames can be removed beforehand to allow the collar to stretch more.

☐ The horse is tied up.

It goes without saying that the harness should be hung up tidily for cleaning, and that the horse should be checked over for injuries or loose shoes before being put away. Any damage to the harness, such as burst stitching round the edge of linings and damaged leather, should be noted and attended to immediately.

The final task after unharnessing the horses is to see to the vehicle. This too must be cleaned and checked over for damage. Movable parts must be greased, the pole or shafts removed and the vehicle put away.

7(2) Putting To and Taking Out

7 (2)i SINGLES

If the horse is to be put to correctly, the vehicle must first be positioned where it is safe for all concerned. The brakes must be in the 'on' position. The whip is laid along the seat with the handle on the left. An assistant should be available to supervise the horse. If the driver has to put the horse to on his own, he should always have the reins so that he can take hold of them if necessary.

The horse, already harnessed, is led up to the vehicle and positioned so that he is facing in the same direction as the vehicle. An assistant holds the shafts approximately at chest height and pushes the vehicle up to the horse so that he is standing between the shafts. If the driver is on his own, he backs the horse into the shafts from in front. Obviously, this method is not to be recommended, especially with young or inexperienced horses. When the horse is standing between the shafts the assistant stands in front of him and ensures that he does not step forward. If the driver is on his own, he must keep hold of the reins with his left hand.

The horse is put to as follows:

☐ The tugs are passed under and around the shafts and through the tug stops. The belly band is then attached first to the left point strap then to the right.*

☐ The traces are attached, right one first, by slipping the leather loop on the end on to the swingle tree, or possibly to the splinter bar if full collar harness is used.†

☐ The kicking strap is attached to the shafts, with the trace running through the loop it makes around the shaft, so that it also acts as a trace bearer.

☐ The kicking strap runs through the backstrap of the crupper behind the point of the hip, and downwards and backwards to the shafts, where it is attached to a metal D. It should not restrict the horse's freedom of movement, but should limit the upward movement. When the horse has been put to there should be room to put a hand on his side on the croup underneath the kicking strap.

☐ When the horse has been put to, the whip checks every detail, paying special attention to the length of the traces. If, when the horse is stood up in his traces, the tug is pushed forward on the saddle, the traces are too short. If the ends of the shafts are level with the back of the shoulder blade, the traces are too long.

---

* This is the method used with French Tilbury tugs (i.e. on a four-wheeled vehicle). With a two-wheeled vehicle, open tugs are used. The shafts are pushed through the tugs as far as the tug stops, and the belly band need not be taken off beforehand.

† In Britain, on single harness the trace usually has a 'crew hole' at the end, which fits over the 'trace hook' on the swingle tree, etc.

100

7(2) ii PAIRS

For driving on the right-hand side of the road, the bigger and stronger of the two horses is usually placed on the right, because every time the vehicle pulls out from the kerb or overtakes, this horse has more work to do: he has to pull the vehicle out from the rough ground at the edge of the road and uphill towards the middle of the road.

When putting to a pair, an assistant should always be present. Only when absolutely quiet, experienced horses are being used can the whip manage on his own. The horses are led carefully up to the vehicle and placed alongside the pole. It must be remembered that they cannot see all around them because of the blinkers, and can easily run into doorways, the vehicle or the pole. They are put to as follows:

☐ The coupling reins are crossed over and attached to the opposite horse. The rein of the horse with the higher head carriage is placed on top. The reins are turned so that the grain side is uppermost.

☐ The pole straps or pole chains are passed through the rings on the collars from the inside outwards, and are left long to start with, with the points not tucked into the keepers.

☐ The end of the right rein is removed from the terret or the point strap on the right-hand (off) horse's harness and thrown over the horses' backs to the left side.

☐ The right outside trace and then the right inside trace are attached to the swingle tree or possibly (with full collar harness) to the roller bolt on the splinter bar.

☐ The left (near) horse's traces are attached in the same order – first the outside, then the inside trace. The outside trace is attached first so that the horse cannot step sideways.

☐ The ends of the reins are buckled together* and tucked out of the way underneath the point strap, with the buckle pointing to the rear.

* Some drivers do not buckle the reins, to avoid getting a foot caught in them.

☐ The last task before the final check is to adjust the pole straps or chains to the correct length. The length should be such that there is an elastic contact between the pole head and the pole strap rings, and the collars or breastcollars are not pulled forwards. The pole head should be about 20cm in front of the horses' breasts, approximately level with the horses' foreheads.

While the horses are being put to the assistant stands in front of them and prevents them from stepping forward. The horses are held by the cheekpieces of their bridles and never by the reins.

If the whip has no alternative but to put the horses in by himself, he should stand them facing a wall. He should buckle the reins together before leading the horses to the vehicle, and be sure to keep hold of them. This is rather tedious, but it is necessary on safety grounds.

After a final check to ensure that the horses are correctly harnessed and put to and are ready to move off, the reins can be taken up and driver and passengers can mount.

Taking out
Both singles and pairs are taken out in the opposite order to that in which they are put to. Whatever operation is being performed, the primary concern is always safety. With a single turnout the whip applies the brake and lays the whip across the box. He then dismounts, keeping the reins in his hand, particularly if he has no assistant to supervise the horse.

The first job is to undo the kicking strap from the shafts. The traces are then taken off and put across the horse's back underneath the back strap. The reins are secured to the left terret. When the shafts have been released from the tugs they should not be dropped on to the ground, but put down carefully.

The horse can then be led into his stable to be unharnessed and attended to.

Pairs are taken out as follows:

□ The reins are unbuckled and thrown over the horses' backs – the groom, passenger or assistant is, of course, standing in front of the horses. The left rein is secured to the terret.

□ The pole straps or chains are let out, but not yet undone completely.

□ The right rein is fastened to the terret.

□ The right horse's traces are undone, first the inside trace then the outside.

□ The left horse's traces are undone, first the inside trace then the outside.

□ The pole straps or chains are undone and placed over the top of the pole.

□ The inside reins (coupling reins) are unfastened from the bits and attached to the opposite horse's throatlatch by passing the points round and back through the keepers.

□ The horses, harness and vehicle are attended to and put away.

7(3) The Driving Whip and its Application

Either a bow-top whip or a drop-thong (Jucker) whip is used, depending on the type (style) of turnout. The bow-top ('swan neck') whip belongs with an English or 'town' turnout, that is, with full collar harness. The drop-thong whip is correct with a country turnout with the horses in breastcollar harness. Bow-top whips should be made from hard, inflexible thorn wood.* A drop-thong whip consists of a straight, firm but pliable stick with a thong attached to the end of it.

Harness horses must be accustomed to the whip right from the beginning of their training. They must learn to respect but not to fear it. The whip should be in the

---

* No particular type of thorn wood is referred to. The reason for using thorn wood is that the nobbly bases of the thorns hold the lash in position on the stick.

driver's hand all the time when he is driving since it is his only means of giving effective forward-driving aids.

The whip is only ever used when the reins are being held in the basic position, i.e. when the right hand is not on the reins. This prevents interference with the horse's mouth. The whip should never make a noise. Cracking the whip is amateurish and upsets the horses. The student must learn to use the whip with an up-and-over movement, using his whole arm, and to lay the thong on exactly where he wants it. Whip aids can only be effective if the horses are wearing blinkers. Whenever more than

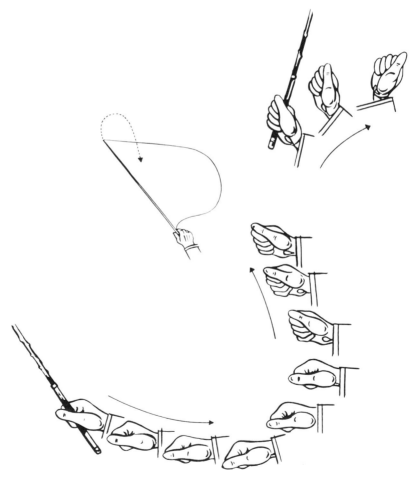

Team whip: catching the thong.

one horse is used there are differences of temperament, and the laziest horse would respond only when it saw the whip raised, while the livelier or excitable horse or horses would be in a state of constant excitement, with their attention permanently focused on the whip.

There are three different kinds of whip aids:

☐ The forward-driving aids.

☐ The collecting aids.

☐ The punishing or correcting aids.

With the *forward-driving aids* the driver yields with his left hand in the direction of the horses' mouths. The

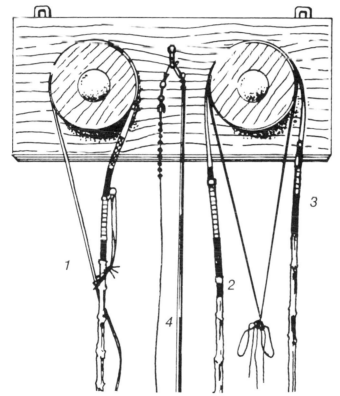

1 Whip hung up correctly. If hung up in this way, the bow-top (quill) will keep its shape.
2 Whip hung too long.
3 Whip hung too short.
4 Drop thong (jucker) whip hung up correctly.

If hung up as in 2 and 3, a bow-top whip loses its shape.

thong of the whip touches the horse who is being sent forward just behind the pad. On turns, only the inside horse should be sent on. If the outside horse is sent on he will cut across into the turn and the horses will turn with their heads looking outwards and their shoulders falling in. The whip is never used between the horses.

In the *collecting aids* the driver keeps a positive contact with the horses' mouths and applies the whip a little behind the pad.

With the *punishing or correcting aids* the driver aims the whip at the horse's shoulder and upper arm, taking care not to lean forward, and at the same time offers positive resistance with his left hand.

When mounting and dismounting the whip is laid across the seat.

If the whip is to keep its shape it must be hung up correctly (see illustration). The thong must be cleaned after use and greased from time to time.

7(4) Moving Off/Halting

When the driver has taken up the reins correctly, and has mounted, picked up the whip and sat down on the right-hand side of the vehicle, the horses should be standing still (as a result of the reins having been taken up correctly) on a light contact with the bit. Even when the groom (on a signal from the driver) has moved away from their heads, the horses must not move off until the driver has told them to do so by feeling their mouths and then yielding the reins again. Refusing to stand still and moving off jerkily are signs of bad training.

Well-brought up and skilfully driven horses quickly learn to stand still in harness and to pull away smoothly. If the horses are young, or if moving off is made difficult owing to bad ground conditions or an excitable horse, the vehicle can be started at a slight angle. Pulling it to one side gets it going and makes it easier to move off straight.

A good driver will always start off at a walk, since this teaches the horses to remain calm.

Before moving off the driver must check that it is safe to do so, and if he is out on the road he must give the appropriate signal with raised whip. The driver must never forget to release the brake before moving off.

The driver indicates to the horses that he wants them to start off by 'feeling the horses' mouths (increasing the contact on the reins), holding this position for a moment, and then yielding. Well-trained horses will move off immediately this aid is given.

To go from a walk to a trot with inexperienced horses, this same aid (in a stronger form) is used. With more advanced horses, who have been taught to go forward and to seek a contact, the aid consists simply of yielding the reins. The horses take this as a signal to trot on, and take a more positive contact of their own.

To halt, the driver transfers the whip to the left hand and applies the brake. His feet should be firmly on the floor of the vehicle just behind the dashboard. He must never lean forward when applying the brake. The brake is then in the 'on' position. The right hand takes back the whip. The hands are in the basic position. If necessary, and if increasing the contact on the horses' mouths is not sufficient to make them halt, the right hand goes down the reins and performs a 'temporary restraining action'. The reins are let out again when the horses have stopped.

Well-trained horses will stop as soon as the contact is increased (when the driver 'feels their mouths'). When driving on the roads, the driver must indicate before stopping. This is done by taking the right hand off the reins and raising the whip vertically. However, he should not stop unless it is safe to do so.

Horses standing still in harness should stand with their weight evenly distributed over all four legs and should maintain a light contact with the bit. The driver should never take his eyes off his horses. If the horses have to remain stationary for any length of time, the groom or passenger should stand in front of them, but without holding the reins. If it becomes necessary for him to hold the horses, he should do so by the cheekpieces of the bridles. For safety's sake the groom should ensure that he is not standing directly in line with the end of the pole.

7(5) Driving in Traffic/Driving in the Country

Nowadays most people who drive horses are used to going out in traffic. When driving a horse-drawn vehicle on a public road the same rules and regulations apply as to other road users, be they pedestrians, cyclists or motorists.

In Germany* the drivers of horse-drawn vehicles are governed by the following laws and acts:

□ The *Strassenverkehrsgesetz* (Road Traffic Act).

□ The *Strassenverkehrsordnung* (Road Traffic Order).

□ The *Strassenverkehrs-Zulassungs-Ordnung* (Road Traffic Licensing Order).

The basic rule which must always be obeyed by all users of the public highway is, as laid down in Paragraph 1 of the German Road Traffic Act:

'All road users must exercise caution at all times and treat others with consideration.

Every road user must behave in such a way that he does not injure or endanger others or cause hindrance or inconvenience beyond that which is unavoidable.'

However, the driver of a horse-drawn vehicle must be aware that in today's fast motor traffic a horse and cart usually constitutes an obstruction and a danger, so that by-roads and quiet streets and roads should be used whenever possible.

Over the last decade people's attitude towards their

* In Great Britain horse drivers must comply with the following: The Road Traffic Act, The Highways Act, The Licensing Act, The Road Vehicle Lighting Regulations.

environment has changed. Any attempt to interfere with nature now meets with fierce resistance, while measures to preserve and safeguard an attractive and ecologically balanced piece of countryside are met with lasting approval. New laws and by-laws, amendments to existing laws, and judgements made in some of the highest courts in the land make it clear that considerable importance is now attached to relaxation in the countryside.

There are, nevertheless, certain legal restrictions on riding and driving through fields and woods. Any person driving a horse-drawn vehicle must therefore make enquiries beforehand as to any regulations which are in force, and must comply with the legal requirements.

In order to travel on the public roads (and this usually applies to woodland and field tracks as well), every vehicle must have its own driver, who must be 'suitable' for the job. The law does not specify what skills the driver should have. A person driving in a town, where the traffic is heavy, will obviously need to be a more accomplished driver than someone who drives only on field and woodland tracks. However, if a driver has proven his skills in a recognised examination, then he should fulfil the requirement of being 'suitable'. In Germany, drivers of horse-drawn vehicles can take the *Fahrerabzeichen* test (in either the single, pair or team and tandem category). Training for the test involves practice and tuition in controlling and driving the turnout, and complying with the legal requirements for driving on a public highway. In that it tests the driver's skill in traffic, the *Fahrerabzeichen* is equivalent for drivers of the German riding qualification, the *Reiterpass*.

7(6) Driving Competition and Examination Requirements (Single and Double Harness)

Competitions are sporting events designed to compare the ability of the whips and the performance of the horses. If the horse is later used in a controlled breeding programme, the results of the competitions will assume special significance, and warrant careful study.

There are various different types and different categories of competition. Apart from 'driver competitions', which test only the skill and technique of the whip with trained horses, there are the following types of competition*:

☐ Long distance driving.

☐ Driven dressage.

☐ Obstacle driving.

☐ Cross-country, including navigating over an unmarked course, but without hazards.

☐ Cross-country over a marked course, and with hazards (marathon).

☐ Driving trials (dressage – with or without presentation – marathon, and obstacle driving).

☐ Combined driving. (A combination of two or more elements, excluding that used in driving trials).

The requirements for individual competitions on a national level are laid down in the German competition rule book, the *Leistungst Prüfungst Ordnung* (LPO) and the *Deutschen Reiterlichen Vereinigung (FN)* notebook, the *Aufgabenheft*.

The rules and details for driving competitions at international level can be found under the heading *Special rules: Driving* in the FEI rule book. The examinations for the German *Fahrerabzeichen* which is awarded

---

* In Germany there are more types of competition than in Great Britain, and most are graded (E = preliminary, A = novice, L = elementary, M = medium, S = advanced). Unlike in Great Britain, the dressage competitions do not always include a presentation phase, especially at the lower levels (preliminary classes never have presentation). The advanced classes have a marathon in accordance with FEI rules, but under German national rules the courses are much shorter at the lower levels (6 to 10km at preliminary). Five-section marathons (permitted only at medium and advanced levels): whereas in Great Britain a five-section marathon consists of trot, walk, fast trot, walk, and trot sections (the last containing the hazards), in Germany there is only one walk section, the hazards are in the fourth section, and the last section is driven at any pace (though at an average speed of 15kph.)

by the Deutschen Reiterlichen Vereinigung, can be taken
in the various zones of the German Federal Republic
upon application to the appropriate competitions and
examinations committee (Kommission für Pferdeleis-
tungsprüfungen) by recognised riding and driving centres
and clubs. There are also *Fahrerabzeichen* awards for
juniors. Grade III (Bronze) and Grade II (Silver) are
awarded on the basis of special examinations, but Grade
I (Gold) is reserved for young drivers who have been
successful in affiliated competitions.

Note: British rules are set out in the *Horse Driving Trials
National Rules* published by the British Horse Society.

7(7) Constructing Obstacle Courses for Driving Competitions

The layout of the course is particularly important. It
should be suitable for the level of training of the horse,
should be as 'flowing' as possible and should contain at
least one change of rein and sections suitable for cantering
and walking, as well as for trotting. The course should
also be laid out so that not all those obstacles of the same
type are together. The course should test the skill of the
driver and the obedience and suppleness of the horses
when performing at speed.

Preparing the course

On the whole, obstacle driving is very much the poor
relation in the world of horse sports: it tends to take
second place, for example to show jumping. Obstacle
driving competitions are often staged at unfavourable
times (often in the morning) and in secondary arenas.
This is not in the interests of the sport, and drivers
deserve to be better rewarded for all the trouble and
expense involved. They should have just as much opportunity to show off their splendid turnouts, upon which
so much time and labour has been expended, as the show
jumpers, whose sport is featured more and more, and

which the audience will merely find boring if it is served up in too-large doses. Competition organisers should be glad of the opportunity to stage an obstacle driving competition, to give the spectators a welcome change from jumping.

Like jumping courses, the building of obstacle courses requires a good deal of time, work and materials, but with a little foresight the organisers can reduce the amount of time required to a minimum – in fact much less than for any jumping course. In order to do so they must make sure that:

☐ There is adequate and continuous liaison between the show jumping course builder and the obstacle driving course builder, and that it begins at an early stage.

☐ Careful consideration is given, also at an early stage, to the question of how best to arrange the programme.

☐ No major alterations to the jumping course are necessary.

☐ The exact line each course is to take is laid down beforehand and strictly adhered to.

☐ The organiser lays on a display, or something similar, while the obstacles are being built.

☐ The arena party is well briefed so that each person knows exactly what he has to do, and the necessary equipment, such as measuring sticks and a list of the widths required for different turnouts, in the right order, is standing ready.

☐ All the materials for building the course are assembled and put ready so that they have to be carried as short a distance as possible.

The whole exercise is a matter of organisation, correct allocation of jobs and team work.

Building the course
The layout of the course depends on whether the area to be used can be cleared completely, or whether the course has to be fitted in around the jumps. In the first case, planning and building the course presents no problems.

In the second, the jumps should be considered as natural obstacles, and the course built around them. It is a good idea to build the obstacles alongside the jumps, and it actually improves the appearance of the course – arenas full of cones and nothing else always look rather bare and desolate, and are confusing for the driver. When there are no jumps, if possible, bushes and flowers – for example potted laurel plants – should be placed at the sides of the obstacles, and everything done to make the course look more attractive. This will be to the benefit of both drivers and spectators.

It is the layout and width of the obstacles which determine the degree of difficulty of the course. The course should be planned in such a way that no obstacle is driven more than once.

If the obstacle driving is to take place between two show jumping classes, the course builder should choose a time when the arena is free (early morning, the day before, or during the lunch break), and should take the arena party and a copy of the course plan and put the course up. If he marks the positions of the obstacles with chalk, lime or sand, he can stack them away at the sides of the jumps and put them up again when required. Each member of the arena party can then be briefed as to his particular job, and told that he must return to the side of the arena after rebuilding and remeasuring a hazard during a round. Only the course builder and his deputies (each responsible for one section of the course) may remain in the arena.

It is essential that when the exact positions of the obstacles are being decided (during the practice run the day before or in the lunch break), the course builder should make sure that they are visible from the judges' box or rostrum. The judges can then see for themselves what is going on, and do not need to rely on the arena party to tell them when a marker has been knocked down, and so on.

If all the preparatory work has been done as described,

Examples of multiple obstacles.

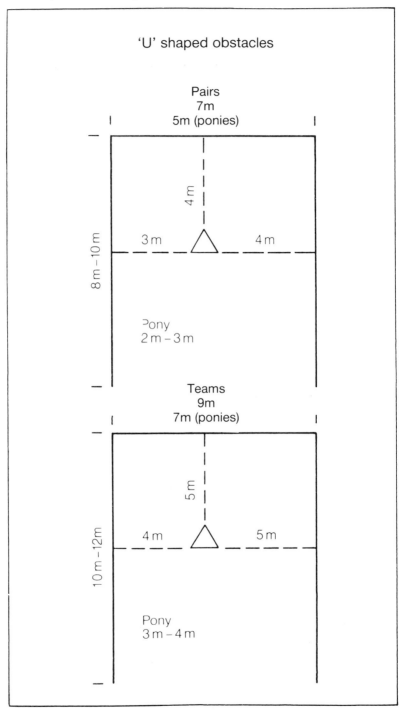

'U' shaped obstacles

Pairs
7m
5m (ponies)

4 m

3 m   4 m

8 m – 10 m

Pony
2 m – 3 m

Teams
9m
7m (ponies)

5 m

4 m   5 m

10 m – 12 m

Pony
3 m – 4 m

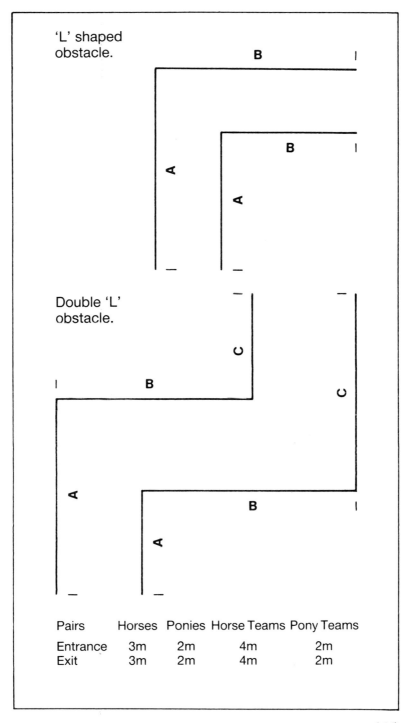

'L' shaped obstacle.

Double 'L' obstacle.

Pairs	Horses	Ponies	Horse Teams	Pony Teams
Entrance	3m	2m	4m	2m
Exit	3m	2m	4m	2m

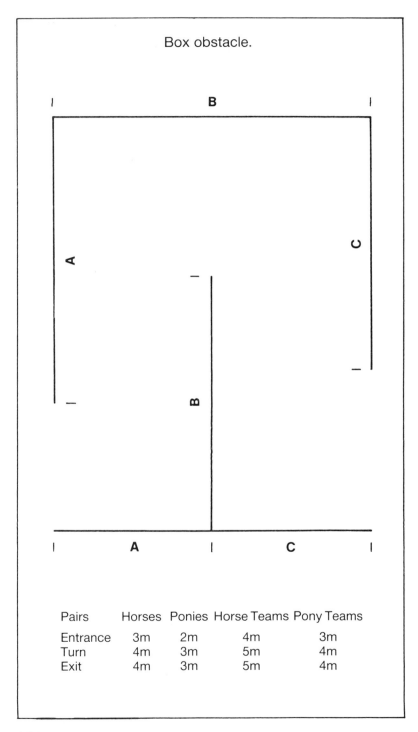

Box obstacle.

Pairs	Horses	Ponies	Horse Teams	Pony Teams
Entrance	3m	2m	4m	3m
Turn	4m	3m	5m	4m
Exit	4m	3m	5m	4m

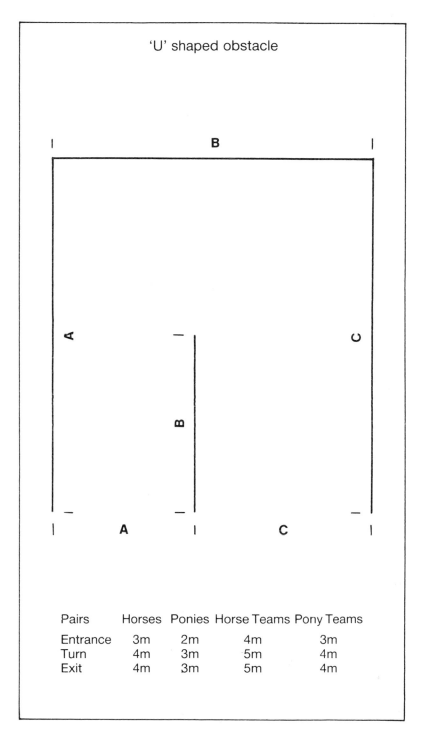

'U' shaped obstacle

Pairs	Horses	Ponies	Horse Teams	Pony Teams
Entrance	3m	2m	4m	3m
Turn	4m	3m	5m	4m
Exit	4m	3m	5m	4m

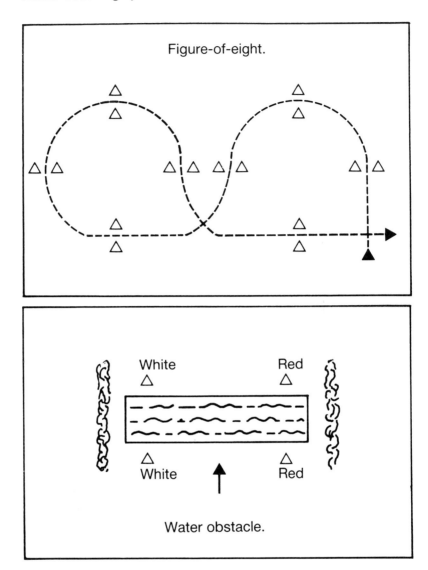

Figure-of-eight.

Water obstacle.

as soon as the jumping competition is finished the obstacle course can be set up in a matter of minutes (during the prize giving for the jumping, or possibly while a display is taking place). During the prize giving for the drivers at the end of the obstacle competition, all the obstacles and cones can be stacked away again next to the jumps. If a vehicle is available to take them away, they can be removed from the arena immediately. Otherwise they can be left until the end of the show.

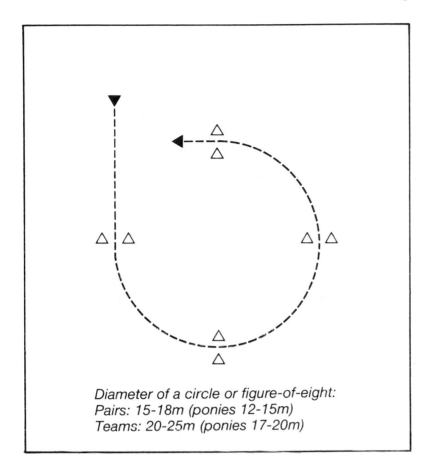

Diameter of a circle or figure-of-eight:
Pairs: 15-18m (ponies 12-15m)
Teams: 20-25m (ponies 17-20m)

The course builder should signal that the course is ready again when the obstacles have been remeasured.

The length of the course may be measured generously. A team has a larger turning circle than a pair. If a great many competitors have time faults, this reflects badly on the course designer.

If the schedule provides for a competition with a run-off, it is a good idea to build a slightly easier course than usual. This will ensure that some competitors go through to the second round, giving the competition an exciting climax. The drive-off should take place over the same course, with the obstacles at the same width, but the 'time allowed' should be adjusted in accordance with the LPO rules.

Unless there is a particularly long, safe run to the exit, the last obstacle should not be facing the exit gate because this can encourage the horses to bolt. The use of a serpentine or a row of obstacles which are off-set from a straight line will ensure that competitors drive slightly more slowly, thus preventing the danger of bolting horses.

Electronic timing equipment should be used wherever possible. If none is available, a signal should be given with a flag as the competitor passes the start.

It is a good idea to appoint deputy course builders, each in charge of a section of the course and of the members of the arena party allocated to that section (how the course is divided up depends on the proportions of the arena). These deputies are responsible for their section of the arena, and they alone should inform the judges of faults which occur in their section. If possible, they should be equipped with two-way radios so that they can deal with any queries from the judges.

One or two pairs of cones should be provided in the practice area, but there is no need to put balls on top of them – experience shows that these tend to become lost.

7(8) The Most Common Faults in Pair Driving

In order to cure driving faults, the driver must first understand what is causing them. He must understand, too, that since each of the reins in his hand acts on both horses, it is impossible for him to tell by feel which of the two horses is doing more of the work of pulling the vehicle, and which of the two has more of a hold on the reins. This information can only be obtained by looking (at the pole, the traces, the pole straps, the reins and the positions of the horses' heads). The driver can then set about curing the fault by adjusting the couplings. For example, if the driver has contact on the reins and both horses' heads are looking to the left, this is a sign that the left horse is going into his traces and doing more of the work than the right horse. Because the left horse is pulling harder on the splinter bar, which is rigid, the pole points permanently to the right. To prevent the vehicle turning to the right, the driver has automatically shortened the left rein, and so caused both horses' heads to turn to the left. To remedy the situation the reins of the horse on the left should be adjusted to bring him further back. If the right-hand horse still hangs back, with his traces loose, he must be sent forward with the whip. Experience shows that the keen horse always settles down when his partner starts to do some of the work. When both horses are pulling equally the pole will be straight and the horses' heads will point straight ahead.

A horse who 'takes a hold' on the bit will not become easier to manage through being bitted more severely, for example, using a curb, or attaching the reins further down the cheek of the curb. On the contrary, a mild bit should be used, otherwise his mouth will become hopelessly hard and unyielding. A constant check should be kept on the mouths of horses who pull, so that any bruising will be noticed immediately.

Paradoxically, bitting the lazier horse more severely is sometimes effective. This is because the whip is used more often on the lazy horse, and with a mild bit he will tend to jump forward, pulling the driver's hand forward and causing the pole to strike the other horse and upset him even more. The result will be that both horses end up going faster and have to be slowed down again.

The most common driver faults
□ Getting up on to the vehicle without checking the harness and the couplings and whether the horses have been put to correctly.
□ Moving off with the brake still on. Not putting the brake on before dismounting and before transitions from a faster to a slower pace.
□ Moving off by jerking the reins, not yielding the reins

sufficiently, or getting the horses 'on the bit' too soon. Whip in the whip holder instead of in the hand.

☐ Leaning forward on the move-off; twisting the upper body so that one shoulder is drawn back; leaning back when halting; sitting with the legs apart.

☐ Intentionally or unintentionally letting the reins slip through the fingers; with the right hand, pulling the reins out through the left hand in an upward direction instead of forwards in the direction of the horses' mouths.

☐ Yielding the reins, but in so doing losing the contact with the horses' mouths.

☐ Pulling on the inside rein when turning (even using the right hand to pull the left rein in left-hand turns).

☐ Slowing down to a walk too late before a right-hand turn,* and failing to shorten the reins sufficiently; not coming back almost to a halt before a 'U' turn in either direction.

☐ Using the whip without taking the right hand off the reins. This interferes with the rein action, and also prevents the driver from touching the horse with the whip at the correct spot, that is just behind the pad.

☐ Making a noise with the whip: making the thong go through the air with a whirring noise and jerking it back so that it makes a noise, or cracking it.

☐ Operating the brake with the whip in the right hand. The whip nearly always catches the off-side horse, and the right hand cannot operate the brake properly.

☐ Not looking round before turning. Looking is just as important as signalling.

Leaning away from the pole

Horses are said to be leaning away from the pole when they use their forefeet to brace themselves against the pole straps and pull outwards away from the pole. One reason for this fault is that the horses are afraid of falling, especially if they have been halted roughly

---

* The right-hand turn refers to a turn made when driving on the right-hand side of the road.

and abruptly (in particular on slippery going). It can also be caused by incorrect adjustment of the coupling reins (both horses going along permanently with their heads turned inwards). To prevent this happening, the reins must always be correctly adjusted for the sizes and widths of the horses. Horses who lean away from the pole are insecure and liable to fall. The driver must be on the look-out for early signs of this fault so that he can act immediately, should it occur, by lengthening the pole straps and putting the brake on slightly to make the horses pull (this slackens off the pole straps). All halts must be carried out so carefully that the horses do not feel the pole straps coming into action. There is less tendency to lean away from the pole once the horses have ceased to feel that they are tied to the pole by the pole straps.

However, usually the best way to cure this fault is to change the two horses round, even if only one of them is leaning away.

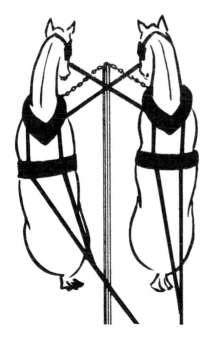
Leaning away from the pole.

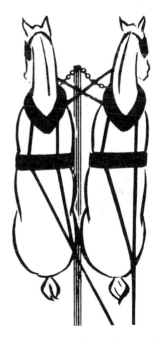
Leaning against the pole.

Leaning against the pole

Horses are said to be leaning against the pole when, on the move, they brace all four feet to the outside so that their bodies touch. This fault usually results from the horses feeling insecure on slippery roads with a pronounced camber, on icy or asphalt surfaces, or on deeply rutted tracks. Each horse tries to push the other away. To prevent this, the turnout should be halted to give the horses a chance to quieten down, and then the journey should be resumed with the horses travelling along the middle of the road, or with the wheels away from the ruts. If the slipping is caused by icy conditions, studs should be used.

Shying

The whip must be able to put himself in his horse's shoes, as it were. Shying is caused by fear due to the horse not being sufficiently accustomed to the sights and sounds he encounters on the roads. It is only occasionally caused by eye defects. Right from the beginning of their training, horses should be encouraged to go forward when they shy, and made to walk slowly past the thing they are frightened of. It is a big mistake to punish a horse for shying: he will be even more frightened the next time because he will be expecting punishment from the whip.

Leaning into the turns

Sometimes horses will throw themselves into the turn. They turn prematurely, with their heads facing outwards, hanging on the outside rein and dropping their inside shoulder into the turn. This bad habit – which is most common when turning to the right – is usually caused by the driver not checking the pace sufficiently and at the right time before the turn, turning too soon, and pulling on the outside rein to avoid cutting the corner. The aids for the turn should therefore be given as late as possible, but very clearly. This will ensure that the horses' heads are flexed in the correct direction, which will prevent them throwing themselves into the turn. Laying the whip on the inside horse in front of his hip will serve as a warning and have the effect of sending the horse forwards so that he pulls the vehicle forwards through the turn instead of cutting across it.

7(9) **Driver Training Plan**

Training must be systematic and progressive, beginning with easy exercises and gradually working up to the more difficult ones. The following plan is divided up into Instruction Units, and can be adjusted and adapted by the trainer according to the circumstances. The lessons should last not less than one hour and not more than two hours without a break. Apart from the subjects listed in the plan, a course in driver training should also include instruction in general horsemastership (see Book 4, *Horse Management*).

1st Instruction Unit
Introduction to the principles of driving.
On the driving apparatus: taking up the reins.
Basic position.
Working position.
Lengthening and shortening both reins from the working position.

2nd Instruction Unit
Revision exercises.
Halts and half-halts: gradual, temporary, prolonged restraining actions.
Explanation of the basic differences between right and left turns.
Harness: harnessing up and unharnessing.

3rd Instruction Unit
Revision exercises.
Harnessing up and unharnessing/harness knowledge.
Exercises on the driving apparatus: schooling position;

intensive practice in the rein holds – working position, schooling position.

4th Instruction Unit
Revision exercises.
Lengthening and shortening individual reins.
Exercises in turning each hand in from the wrist (rounding the wrists).
Carriages.
Practical driving along straight lines.

5th Instruction Unit
Harnessing up, putting to and taking out, unharnessing.
Exercises on the driving apparatus: turns with the reins in the schooling position.
Use of the whip: practice on dummy.
Practical driving along straight lines.

6th Instruction Unit
Instruction in the different ways of coupling the reins and the measurements used; exercises in coupling the reins.
Practical driving along straight lines.

7th Instruction Unit
Revision exercises.
Explanation of the different parts of the harness; different types of harness and styles of turnout.
Practical driving in the school/driving turns.

8th Instruction Unit
Revision exercises.
Practical driving/changes of pace.
Driving turns with the reins in the basic position.

9th Instruction Unit
Revision exercises.
Practical driving in traffic.
Long reining.
Lecture on training young horses to harness.

126

10th Instruction Unit
Revision exercises.
Practical driving in traffic and in the school with tight turns.
Long reining.

11th Instruction Unit
Revision exercises.
Obstacle driving, at a slow pace to begin with.

12th Instruction Unit
Revision exercises.
Obstacle driving at a slow pace.

13th Instruction Unit
Revision exercises.
Driving dressage tests in the school.
Obstacle driving at a faster pace.

14th Instruction Unit
Revision exercises.
Dressage exercises.
Obstacle driving at a fast pace.
Driving in traffic.

15th Instruction Unit
Revision exercises.
Exercises on everything learned.

SECTION TWO
Training of the Driving Horse in Single and Double Harness

1. Aims and Requirements

When training a horse to harness, the aim is to produce an animal who is steady even in the heaviest traffic, and one who is quiet but at the same time forward-going and a pleasure to drive.

Today's harness horse is not as a rule considered mainly as a means of pulling or transporting goods or agricultural implements. He is now used mainly in the field of leisure activity, either for recreation and relaxation or in sport. If the horse is to fulfil the requirements made of him, he will need a trainer who is an expert in this field. Pony owners tend to think that anybody can teach a pony to pull a cart, and that anyone can drive him. This is quite wrong and can be highly dangerous. Anyone who intends to train a horse (or pony) to harness must first learn how to harness up and put to correctly and should practise driving quiet, experienced horses. He must also possess an adequate knowledge of horses.

1(1) The Physical and Mental Qualities Required in a Harness Horse

The physical qualities required in a driving horse are basically the same as those required in a riding horse. The most important criterion for judging a driving horse is performance. Conformation will provide some guidelines in this respect, but factors such as health, temperament, boldness, stamina, willingness and food utilisation (is the horse a good or bad 'doer'?) are also vital.

Of particular importance in driving are the head and eye, the bearing and carriage, and the way the horse behaves and reacts to his surroundings. In addition, a driving horse needs to have powerful, ground-covering paces. Those splendid animals of the Oldenburg coach-horse type, who used to pull smart town carriages in days gone by, and were of East Friesian or Holstein origin, have now disappeared. However, the German Riding Horses from the various regions of Germany (used for competition driving) are just as well suited, if not more so, to driving as the old coach horses were. The many breeds of pony, which have been much 'improved' over the past few decades, also make excellent driving horses, and are of inestimable value, especially for 'leisure' driving. Hackneys are not so suitable for the practical driver, though they can be very impressive, with their high head carriage and extravagant knee action.

One point worth mentioning in connection with knee action – which fascinates even those people who know nothing about horses – is that it is the way a horse puts his feet down, not how he picks them up, which determines how sure-footed he is.

As well as having knowledge of driving, the trainer needs to know how an animal's mind works, otherwise he risks overfacing the horse both physically and mentally. If the trainer does not proceed with tact and judgement, he will unbalance the horse's mental equilibrium, and the damage will take months, if not years, to put right. He will also cause physical damage, particularly to the horse's limbs, and premature breakdown.

A driving horse needs to be mentally stable, to have a good character, and to be implicitly obedient because, especially in a team, he is not under such close control as a horse who is being ridden. Like any animal, a horse will always tend to act in accordance with his primitive reflexes and only the trainer who has some basic knowledge of equine psychology will succeed in his task. More information on this subject can be found in Books 1 and 4 of this series, *The Principles of Riding* and *Horse Management*.

1(2) Where to Train and the Different Stages in Training

A driving horse can only be trained correctly where there is peace and quiet and where it is possible to observe the necessary safety rules. It is wrong to choose heavy going to begin with, simply on the grounds that the horse is supposed to be learning how to pull. In fact, heavy going will have the reverse effect, since young horses soon start jibbing if they are overfaced. Until the horse is used to the work, the best place to train is in an indoor school. Subsequently, a large arena or a field, without barbed wire fencing, may be used.

The training is divided up into the following stages: The first stage consists in accustoming the horse to the harness and equipment. The second stage is to improve the horse's suppleness by working him on the lunge and in long reins. The horse is then familiarised with pulling, by making him draw a light sledge on long traces. Only when this has been achieved can the horse be gradually familiarised with the task of pulling a vehicle, which he should do alongside another, very experienced horse (a 'schoolmaster'). When this stage has been successfully completed, the horse may go on to be trained in single harness. The final stage is the specialised training in the different types of sport.

1(3) Accustoming the Horse to the Harness and Equipment

Nowadays most horses become used to people when they are foals. Having a headcollar put on, being tied up, and having their feet picked up and handled is nothing new to them. Something else which helps when it comes to training a horse to harness is the fact that many young horses sent for training are already used to wearing a saddle and to being ridden.

Breastcollar harness is best for accustoming a horse

to wearing harness. It is light, can be adjusted to fit any horse and fulfils the purpose of getting the young horse used to the pressure exerted on its breast when it pulls.

Great care should be taken when familiarising the horse with the crupper. Very sensitive horses should first be given a good work-out on the lunge so that they are becoming tired by the time the crupper is put on. The first time it is fitted there should be assistants present to divert the horse's attention, to lift up one of his forelegs or take other safety precautions. The horse will find it easier to accept the crupper if he is used to his groom lifting his tail every time he grooms him and cleaning his dock with a sponge, water and a cloth.

It is not enough simply to put the harness on: the horse must also become used to moving about while wearing it. This should be done at first by leading the horse in hand. Pieces of harness should not be allowed to hang down unnecessarily and hit the horse's legs, since this will irritate and annoy him. The more time the trainer spends in the early days getting the horse used to the harness, the easier the later training will be.

It is a good idea to use an ordinary riding bridle in the early stages of training, and to use the driving bridle with blinkers only when the horse is used to the harness and to the feel of the long reins against his legs.

Familiarising the horse with the harness will take only a few days if the trainer goes about it quietly and patiently.

2. Training

The efficiency of a turnout consisting of more than one horse depends on the efficiency of each horse. For maximum efficiency each horse needs to have been individually and expertly trained. A horse's reliability in harness depends on his having been knowledgeably, quietly and patiently handled and trained to harness as a youngster. Faults which develop during this period can seldom be eradicated.

The tactics used in training, and the safety precautions taken, depend on the horse's temperament. Quiet, expert handling is the first requirement for successful training. Excitement, shouting and running should be avoided. Force should not be used on a horse who is excitable or difficult. Any horse can be trained with patience, provided the trainer knows how to assess and overcome any problems which arise. However, no one can force a horse to pull.

It is a good idea to begin the training of a harness horse by first teaching him to carry a rider. A horse who is used to a saddle and the weight of a rider will be quieter and will raise fewer objections when he is trained to harness.

As with a riding horse, the aims in training the driving horse are as follows:

Rhythm
The walk or trot strides remain perfectly even (in length and duration), even when the tempo alters. Cantering is only occasionally required of a harness horse.

Losgelassenheit (suppleness and looseness)
Muscles can only be said to be working efficiently when they have an adequate blood supply (i.e. when

they are 'warmed up') and when they are contracting and relaxing correctly in accordance with the task the horse has to perform. When all the necessary physical and psychological conditions have been fulfilled, and this has been achieved, the horse is said to be in a state of *Losgelassenheit*.

Contact

A horse going fowards in *Losgelassenheit* stretches forwards by extending his neck and back, and takes a contact with the bit, and so, via the reins, with the rider's hands (but without leaning on them).

Schwung (impulsion and elasticity)

Schwung is the energetic impulse, created by the powerfully working hind legs, passing into the forward movement. The result is an elastically swinging back.

Straightness

If full use is to be made of the power developed in the hindquarters, and one-sided wear and tear is to be avoided during the horse's driving career, the horse must be straight throughout his entire length, that is, along his longitudinal axis.

Collection

Together with the general suppling effect of the training, the above-mentioned qualities enable the horse to bend the joints of his hindquarters and thus transfer more of his weight on to them. This lightens the forehand and allows the forelegs to be lifted higher. The horse is also able to balance himself better in tight turns.

2(1) Work on the Long Reins

Before work on the long reins is begun, the horse must first be taught to lunge, as described in Book 1, *The Principles of Riding*. Work on the long reins prepares the horse for the rein aids and teaches him what they mean. Also, the outside rein running around the hind legs just above the hocks prepares the horse for the contact of the harness, especially the traces. Ticklish horses, who would otherwise kick out and be a danger to the vehicle and the passengers, can be safely put to if they have first been familiarised with the long reins. Even horses who seem quiet and easy going occasionally kick when they are being long reined. Hence no horse should be put to without first being long reined, and this work should be so thorough that the horse will not kick once he has been put to. Re-training horses who have been put to too early is very time consuming, and bad habits are extremely difficult to eradicate.

For long reining, as for lungeing, the horse's forelegs should be bandaged, and brushing boots should be fitted on the hind legs, especially if the horse is shod. Other equipment is described below.

Horse suitably equipped for his first lesson in long-reining.

The bridle

In the first stages of training an ordinary riding bridle with a plain, thick snaffle is used, then a driving bridle and snaffle, but without blinkers to start with. Blinkers should not be used for long reining because they can cause dizziness. They restrict the horse's field of vision so that when working on a circle he can see only the area immediately in front of him. The horse should be familiarised with the blinkers slowly. The time to fit them is when the horse is first put to alongside the 'schoolmaster'.

The harness

At the beginning of training it is a good idea to use breastcollar harness, but the horse must also learn eventually to wear full collar harness.

The traces are removed from the breastcollar. The tug trace buckles of the breastcollar or the hame tug buckles of the (full) collar should be fastened to the point strap of the pad or saddle, which should be fitted with a crupper.

The hame tug buckle or tug trace buckle should lie against the chest on a level with the shoulder joint (point of shoulder). A large ring – at least 5 to 6cm in diameter, but preferably 10cm – is attached at the point where the tug buckle joins on to the false belly band on either side. The long reins each pass through one of these rings (one inside, one outside).

The long reins

The total length of the two reins should be approximately 16 to 17m. They are attached to the bit rings by means of buckles or spring clips.

It is a good idea to have the long reins made up all in one piece, without a buckle in the middle, because the buckle gets in the way. Furthermore, it makes things easier if the first 2m or so of the reins at the bit end are made of rolled leather, because they will then slide through the rings on the pad, saddle or roller (breaking roller) more easily. An ordinary lunge rein joined to a rein from a set of single harness can be used as a substitute for a pair of long reins, although the join will get in the way.

Lungeing/long-reining whip

A whip of the type used for lungeing is suitable for long reining.

For long reining, the trainer should be dressed in such a way that he can move freely. Leather gloves are recommended. The area used for long reining should be in a quiet location. When starting the work on the long reins it is best to have an assistant to lead the horse on the circle. Preferably – if there is room – the assistant should be on the outside of the horse so that he does not get in the trainer's way. If necessary, the horse may be led by a rein attached to a headcollar fitted underneath the bridle, instead of by the long rein.

The trainer should stand in the middle of the circle. Ideally, he should hold both reins in one hand, thus leaving the other free to use the whip correctly. However, with a young horse in the early stages of training it will be necessary to hold a rein in each hand and to have an assistant to control the whip. Once this stage is past, holding the reins in the basic position used for driving, has been found to give good results.

When long reining to the left, the reins are held in the left hand, with the left rein running over the index finger at the knuckle, and the right between the second and third fingers. If the ends of the reins are too long, they can be hooked up on the little finger. The right hand controls the whip, the end of which points towards the horse's hind leg. As in driving (basic and schooling positions), the right hand may also assist with the right rein if necessary.

When long reining to the right (on the right rein), the whip is held in the left hand. The reins are held in the right hand, with the right rein between the second and third fingers and the left rein between the thumb and

Long-reining. Here the horse is wearing a breastplate or light breastcollar.

Long-reining: position of the outside rein.

index finger, running down through the whole hand. Here again, the end of the reins may be hooked over the little finger, and the left hand may assist as required.

When first teaching the horse to long rein, it is sometimes advisable to run the inside rein straight back to the hand, as in ordinary lungeing, rather than running it through the ring on the pad or the rein terret on the collar. The horse must be accustomed to the outside rein gradually. Again, it is a good idea to run it initially straight over the back and not to put it round the hindquarters until the end of the lesson. In this way, the horse will not take long to become used to it. If he does kick out at first, he should not be punished by being jabbed in the mouth. Instead, the trainer should simply ensure that he continues to go forward, and that he does not get the outside rein between his hind legs. Once the horse is used to being long reined, both the outside and the inside reins can be put through the rings on the pad and the hame terrets on the collar, or the terrets on the neck strap of the breastcollar.

The trainer walks round in a small circle in the centre. He should face, and look in, the direction of the movement. The outside rein, which comes round the back of the horse's hind legs, should never be tight so that it restricts the horse's movement. The horse is steered with the inside rein; the outside rein has a regulating effect, like the regulating outside leg ('guard leg') in riding. When the horse is moving, the outside rein should not be allowed to drop below the level of the hocks.

When the horse has achieved some degree of proficiency on the long reins, changes of rein may be attempted, beginning with changes *out of the circle* (as in a figure-of-eight), and later progressing to changes *through the circle* (an S-shape through the middle of the circle) as described in Book 1, *The Principles of Riding*. At first, changes of rein should be driven at a walk, but later a short, balanced trot may be employed.

When driving a change of rein on the long reins, the aids can be the same as for driving the same figure from the vehicle, with the reins in the schooling position. However, changing the whip from one hand to the other requires a little practice.

To begin with, work on the long reins should not exceed twenty minutes. Later in the horse's long-rein training, the trainer may move behind him and drive him along straight lines in the school.

For the rein-back the trainer stands behind the horse, shortens the reins and quietly asks the horse to take one or two steps backwards on a straight line. If he refuses, the trainer steps to the side and 'mobilises' the hindquarters by using the outside rein, as in leg yielding. The resulting sideways step can then be converted into a backward step by asking ('taking') with both reins when the leg is in the air. Any tendency to 'run' backwards should be corrected. Always praise the horse when he reins back correctly.

When working on straight lines, impulsion should be maintained by frequently sending the horse forward on a circle at an energetic trot.

Ten to fourteen days' intensive long reining should be sufficient to prepare the horse to be put to the vehicle.

2(2) Putting To and Training with the Vehicle

Once the horse has been familiarised by long reining, with the harness and the contact of parts of the harness on his hind legs, he may be introduced to the task of pulling. Here, too, the safety of the handlers and the peace of mind of the horse are most important, so it is advisable to extend the traces by attaching one or more lengths of strong rope to the end of them. Two or more assistants then hold on to the ropes and the horse is asked to pull them. At first, however, they do not brace themselves against the ropes. When the horse will pull this light weight, the pull can be increased by asking the assistants to lean back against the traces. Frequent breaks should be given and the horse must be praised and rewarded with food. Pulling four people who are bracing themselves against the traces is the equivalent of pulling a weight of 40 to 50cwt. The horse should never be allowed to lose confidence by being overfaced.

When the trainer feels that the horse is coping well with his work, he can go on to the next stage, which is harnessing the horse by the extended traces to a sledge. The drawbar on the front of the sledge should be fairly wide, so that the traces are as wide apart as possible at the ends. The recommended width is approximately 1.50m.

These early lessons should always take place in an indoor school or in a larger but enclosed area. At first the horse needs to work on fairly long straight lines. The length of the lessons can be extended to about an hour. When the horse shows no hesitation in going forward into his collar, and takes no notice of the traces touching it, he can progress to pulling a carriage. A solidly built, safe, free-moving vehicle is essential. On no account must the driver's seat be too low, which would be dangerous for him and would not allow him to observe the horse. These lessons should take place on a soft but not deep ground and the horse should be harnessed alongside a really steady schoolmaster.

A breaking cart is recommended, but whatever vehicle is used, it must have a fixed splinter bar and swingle tree, because this is the only system which enables the driver to control the distribution of work. Initially, the aim is not to get the horse used to pulling heavy weights, but to train him to go along in front of the vehicle and to accept being attached to it. At first the schoolmaster should do the pulling, and the pupil's share of the work should be limited to keeping the vehicle straight. The older horse's traces may be slightly shorter than normal, and those of the young horse slightly longer. Similar adjustments may be made to the pole straps.

The use of an evener (an extra pivoting bar between

Young horse pulling a safe, suitable type of sledge.

the fixed draw bar and the swingle trees) can have unde-
sirable effects because when one horse moves forward the
other horse is pulled back by the action of the evener. If
the second horse then jumps forward, a see-sawing movement results, which can be very unnerving, particularly
for the young horse.

It is also a good idea to stable the schoolmaster and his
pupil in adjacent boxes or stalls for a few days beforehand
so that they will have had a chance to get to know each
other.

Immediately before he is put to for the first time, the
youngster should be given a thorough work-out pulling
the sledge. The schoolmaster should already have been
put to, on the left of the pole, and should stand waiting.

143

To begin with, the youngster should be put on the right, so that the driver does not touch him on the croup with the reins as he mounts* and thus make him kick. Later on, when he goes out on the roads, if he is on the right he will be further away from overtaking and approaching traffic, and may also be on softer ground.† However, at some stage in his training every horse must learn to go on the left, to prevent one-sidedness and to straighten him.

When putting to for the first time, good results have been obtained with the following method. The youngster, wearing a snaffle bridle over an ordinary stable headcollar, is brought alongside the pole and tied by a rope attached to his headcollar to the pole strap ring of his neighbour. It must be ensured, however, that he is able to hold his head straight, i.e. that his head is not bent towards that of his neighbour. The coupling (inside) reins are then attached to the bits and the pole straps are fastened. Finally the traces are attached in the order already explained: first the outside one, then the inside. It is a good idea to have another helper praising the horse and distracting him with food. The driver must mount very carefully.

If the horse stands quietly, the driver should then get him used to his movements on the box and on the vehicle while it is at a standstill. When he moves off he should be slightly to the left, with the helper still at the young horse's head. By this method the older horse does the pulling and steers the young one smoothly in the direction of the movement with the pole strap. On no account must the helper on the ground hold the horse tightly with the rope or lunge rein. His job is simply to ensure that the horse does not turn his head towards his neighbour, take fright at the pole, or try to run away. The lessons should not be too long at first, and the horses should always be taken out (from the vehicle)

---

* In Germany the driver mounts on the left.
† When driving on the right.

144

facing away from home so that the young horse stays as calm as possible.

The early lessons should be conducted at a walk, and the horse must be given plenty of exercise beforehand on the long reins or under saddle. The walk work calms the horse and gives him confidence. It is better to spend a few days on this stage and finish up with a steady, safe driving horse, than to try to go quickly and produce a horse who is nervous and unreliable for years afterwards.

The horse must receive proper care after the lesson: a sore horse will start to resist. Each time the harness is taken off, all the areas of the body which come in contact with it must be sponged down very carefully with cold water. If sore places are revealed, the horse should not be worked again in harness until the sores have healed completely and are no longer sensitive to pressure. Even with experienced horses, careful attention should be paid to the areas underneath the collar or breastcollar.

Daily lessons with the young horse can become progressively longer. The right moment to put on the winker/blinker bridle and to start accustoming the horse to going out on the roads, and eventually in traffic, depends entirely on the horse's progress and is at the discretion of the trainer.

Even when the horse is quite happy pulling the vehicle, if the harness is changed, for example from breastcollar to full collar, or the horse is changed over to the other side of the pole, the trainer must proceed with extreme caution.

Not until the horse will work perfectly steadily alongside the schoolmaster should the idea be entertained of driving him in single harness. Here, too, certain preparatory work is recommended. The pressure of the shafts in the turns is a particular source of trouble with young horses, and something they should become used to before they are driven as singles. A pair of shafts attached to a sledge will do the job, or the horse may be led dragging a pole on either side.

145

Suggested plan for training a horse to harness

Day 1
Carefully fit the harness and accustom the horse to long reining.
Walk and trot work on the circle.
Loosening up.

Day 2
Walk and trot work on the circle.
Loosening up.
Long-rein work at the halt (for example, touching the horse all over with the long reins to familiarise him with them. Lateral and direct flexion work could also be included).

Day 3
As on day 2.

Day 4
Walk and trot work on the circle.
Loosening up.
Work on the long reins on straight lines. School figures on the long reins.
Teaching the horse to obey the 'yielding' rein aids.
Long rein work at the halt, as on day 2.

Day 5
Long-rein work as on days 1 to 4.
Accustoming the horse to the whip: touching him with the whip/running the whip over him, etc.

Day 6
Long-rein work as on day 4.
Rein-back.

Day 7
Long-rein work as on days 1 to 6.
Accustoming the horse to noises and the whip.

Day 8
Long-rein work as on days 1 to 7.

Teaching the horse to pull, using extended traces.

Day 9
As for day 8.
Accustoming the horse to different types of harness (full collar).

Day 10
As for day 9.

Day 11
As for days 1 to 10.

Day 12
As for day 11.

Day 13
As for day 11.

Day 14
As for day 11.
Putting to, with a steady older horse, in the breaking cart. Walk and gentle trot for about twenty minutes.

Day 15
As for day 14, the horse having been worked in beforehand.

Day 16
As for day 15, gradually asking the horse to pull more, and for longer.

Days 17 to 19
As for day 15.

Day 20
The same work outside along the lanes, gradually accustoming the horse to traffic.

Days 21 to 25
As for day 20, at some point switching the horses round and using a different type of harness (full collar/breastcollar).

Days 26 to 30
As for days 21 to 25, at some point accustoming the horse to the shafts after his lesson in the pairs vehicle/leading the horse in the shafts.

Days 31 to 40
Driving in double and single harness, gradually increasing the demands.
Frequent driving across country and in traffic.

Further exercises as required.

2(3) Driving in Competitions and Sporting Events with Single Turnouts and Pairs

Horses to be used in driving competitions must be quiet in harness, that is, they must be sufficiently well trained that they may be put straight in and driven away. They must be obedient and equally well trained on either rein.

To compete with a chance of being placed, not only must the horse have been carefully schooled, but he must also be fit. So, too, must his driver. As with riding horses, different levels of fitness are required for different disciplines. The highest level is that required for roads and tracks and cross-country (with hazards)*.

Before taking part in the higher level competitions,† in addition to correct schooling the horse must undergo a programme of special fitness training. The duration of this training depends on the level of the competition, but it should be a minimum of six weeks. For the weeks leading up to a competition, a feeding schedule should be worked out and adhered to, and care should be taken to ensure that the horse's shoes are in good order for the competition, his mane pulled, and so on.

---

* These are individual competitions in Germany, as well as being phases of a 'driving trial', as in Britain.
† In Germany the novice courses are very short and easy, unlike those in Britain, which require the horse to be quite fit.

148

The requirements for the different types and levels of competition are laid down in the German competition rule book, the *Leistungs-Prüfungs-Ordnung* (LPO) and the *Aufgabenheft* (booklet containing the tests) of the Deutsche Reiterliche Vereinigung, as well as in the rule book of the International Equestrian Federation (FEI), in the section on driving.

SECTION THREE

Training for Driving
a Team, Tandem, etc

1. Types of Turnout

This section deals with various turnouts other than singles and pairs. It is possible for a driver to have control over any type of turnout up to and including a six-in-hand, and to take it out safely in traffic. Beyond this number – that is, turnouts consisting of more than six horses – the driver is not in a position to be safely in control in traffic.

Depending on the number of horses used, and their positions, the following types of turnout are recognised:
☐ Four-in-hand (team)
☐ Five-in-hand
☐ Six-in-hand
☐ Tandem
☐ Randem
☐ Unicorn
☐ Troika

1(1) Four-in-Hand or Team

A four-in-hand consists of two pairs of horses, one in front of the other. The two horses immediately in front of the vehicle are known as the wheelers, and the two in front of them as the leaders. As with pairs, there are two types of turnout:
☐ English or town turnout with full collar harness.
☐ Country or Jucker (Hungarian) turnout with breast-collar harness or special Hungarian-style harness.
To be correct, the turnout should consist of four horses who are as similar as possible. The leaders should be slightly finer and have more dash and sparkle than the wheelers, though they should not be smaller. Greys and blacks are acceptable in the same team; they should be

in diagonally opposite pairs (near leader grey, off leader black, near wheeler black, off wheeler grey, or vice versa).

The weight of the vehicle should correspond to the type of horses. It should not be too heavy, but neither should it be too light. Suitable vehicles for four-in-hands are brakes, coaches, mail phaetons, Hungarian Jucker waggons, and waggonettes. It is important that the box seat should be high, so that the whip has a good view of the horses.

1(2) Six-in-Hand

A six-in-hand is a heavier type of turnout, and the harness used should reflect this. The turnout consists of three pairs of horses, one in front of the other, driven in full collar harness to a heavy and sufficiently high carriage. The best horses for this purpose are coach-horse types.

1(3) Tandem

A tandem consists of two horses, one in front of the other. The 'shaft horse', which is the one immediately in front of the vehicle, may be of a heavier type. The leader should be finer and particularly onward-going. A well-balanced two-wheeled tandem cart is a suitable vehicle. As in driving a team, it is important that the driver's seat should be high up. The 'shaft horse' (wheeler) should preferably wear full collar harness. The leader may wear breastcollar harness, though full collar is also acceptable.

1(4) Random

A random consists of three horses, one behind the other. The type of harness and choice of vehicle are the same as for the tandem.

153

1(5) Unicorn

The unicorn is a type of turnout which is not often seen. It consists of a pair, with a third horse harnessed in front as in a tandem. Any vehicle which is suitable for a pair will be satisfactory for a unicorn.

2. Equipment for Teams, Tandems, etc.*

Certain additional items of equipment are necessary for these turnouts (both on the harness and on the vehicle). Otherwise, anything said in the section about pairs also holds good for these turnouts.

2(1) Four-in-Hand

Irrespective of whether the horses are wearing breast-collar or full collar harness, the following extra equipment is necessary for the wheelers:

☐ One bridle terret each, buckled into the throatlatch on the outside of the bridle. The lead reins (leaders' reins) pass through these terrets.

☐ One centre terret each on the pad (in the position occupied by the bearing-rein hook on pairs' harness). These terrets, too, are for the lead reins, making it easy to see which rein is which.

The pole head on a team vehicle must have a hook on it, to which the lead bars are attached. This hook, or 'crab', has a leather strap running across the opening so that the wheelers' bits cannot become caught on it.

It is even more important with a team than with a pair that the end of the pole head can turn: if one horse falls this will help prevent the horse being injured and the pole being broken.

The harness for the leaders does not differ greatly from a set of pair harness. However, the usual Achenbach pair reins are not suitable for the wheelers of a team, because

---

* In Britain far more alternatives, both in types of vehicle and types of harness, are acceptable. Many variations on the harness described are in common use, such as fixed bridle terrets (rosette terrets or roger rings) as opposed to the 'drop' terrets mentioned in this section.

Bridle terrets for four-in-hand, six-in-hand, tandem and randem.

the coupling buckles are too close to the hand, and when the reins are held in certain positions the buckles finish up actually in the hand.

On correct team wheeler reins, the middle hole is further forward – only 2.45m from the bit instead of 2.90m as with pair reins. The length of the inside reins is 2.57m. As for pairs, the total length of each outside rein is 4.20m.

On the lead reins the middle hole is 2.15m from the outside of the bit, and the inside reins are only 2.27m long, instead of 3.02m as in pair reins. They are shorter so that the couplings are well clear of the wheelers. The total length of each lead rein is 7.10 to 7.20m. On both lead reins the last splice (join) must be 1.80m from the rear end, otherwise it is impossible to measure out the reins accurately before mounting, and thus impossible to move off in an orderly manner.

Improvised reins are never successful. It is impossible to drive a four-in-hand correctly without proper Achenbach team reins. The leaders are attached to the vehicle by the lead bars (a main bar and two single bars). The lead bars used with a town turnout are heavier than those used with a Hungarian turnout.

The whip used with a four-in-hand is different from that used with a pair. With full collar harness (English or

Four-in-hand reins.

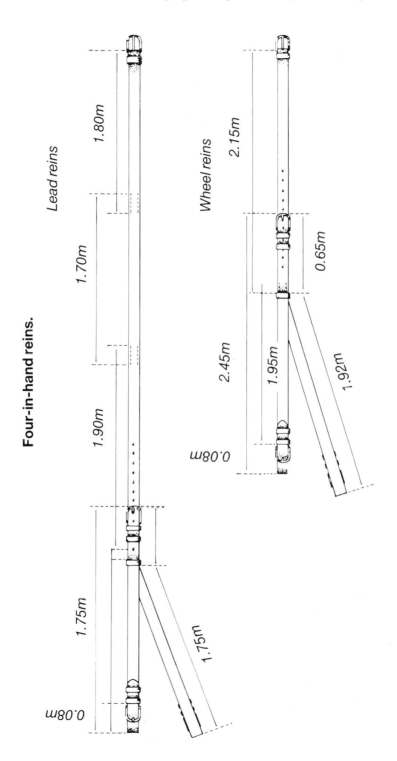

Lead reins

Wheel reins

1.80m

2.15m

1.70m

0.65m

1.90m

2.45m

1.95m

1.92m

0.08m

1.75m

1.75m

0.08m

any type of town turnout), it is stylistically correct to use a bow-top whip with a stick 1.50m long, and thong and bow-top (quill) together measuring 3.80 to 4.00m. With breastcollar and country turnouts, a drop-thong whip is used, with a stick 1.50m long and a thong 3.80 to 4.00m, as with a bow-top whip. It is important that the whip is the proper length so that the driver is in a position to give the necessary whip aids to the leaders. More on this subject can be found in Part 1, section 7.3, *The whip and its application.*

Because teams, tandems, etc, are longer than pairs, the driver needs to sit higher to be able to see all the horses. For this reason, vehicles designed especially for this type of turnout are equipped with a sloping, wedge-shaped cushion to raise the driver's seat.

2(2) Six-in-Hand

Harness and equipment for a six-in-hand is similar to that used with a four-in-hand. The total length of the lead reins, however, is 10.20m, with the coupling reins 2.27m long. Between the middle pair of horses, the 'swing pair', there is an additional pole, the 'swing pole', which is attached to the wheelers' pole hook below the main bar. The swing pole is carried by the swing horses by means of elasticated pole bearers, which buckle on to the inside trace buckles. Like the wheel pole, the swing pole has a crab, and rings for the attachment of the pole straps. The leaders are attached to this pole by the lead bars, which should if possible be lighter than those used for the swing horses.

To make it possible to see which rein is which, each of the wheelers' pads has a double terret, so that the swing reins and the lead reins go through separate rings.

Left: Pad for six-in-hand wheeler with terrets for swing and lead reins.

2(3) Tandem

There are two important differences between tandem harness and normal single harness. First, the shaft horse (wheeler), who should if possible always wear full collar harness, has special tug buckles with an eye on them for the attachment of the two lead bars, which are known as tandem bars. Bars* are recommended for technical reasons. Second, also for technical reasons, the leader's pad is slightly different from an ordinary single harness pad. The point straps form loops through which the traces are passed to stop them crossing over the horse's back when turning. Alternatively, the pad may have a fixed leather loop on each side. Furthermore, the width of the leader's pad should be approximately 9cm, whereas that of the wheeler should be approximately 15cm.

As has already been mentioned, a tandem leader may wear breastcollar harness. For a tandem, a terret with a roller bar across the centre (so-called 'tandem terret'†) on the wheeler's pad is essential because of the closeness of the reins. The bridle of the wheeler has similar terrets to those used for a four-in-hand.

A tandem wheeler should always wear a breeching, though care must be taken to ensure that there are no straps or tongues of buckles on which the lead reins could become caught.

For preference, a high tandem cart should always be used with this sort of turnout. It is particularly important that it should be well balanced. Tandem carts with the centre of gravity too far back (tail heavy) make the shaft horse's work much harder and are unsafe for the driver.

---

* Rather than long traces attached directly to the wheeler's tug buckles.
† The dividing bar may also have a roller on it (roller bar terret). In Britain the lead reins are not usually passed through the wheeler's collar terrets.

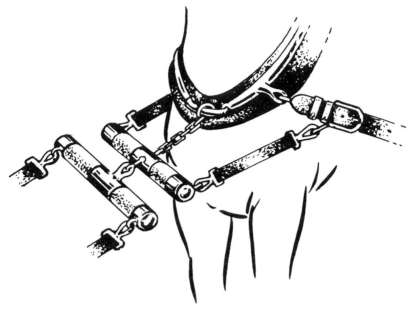

Double bars ('tandem bars').

Tandem leader pad with loops on the sides for the traces to pass through.

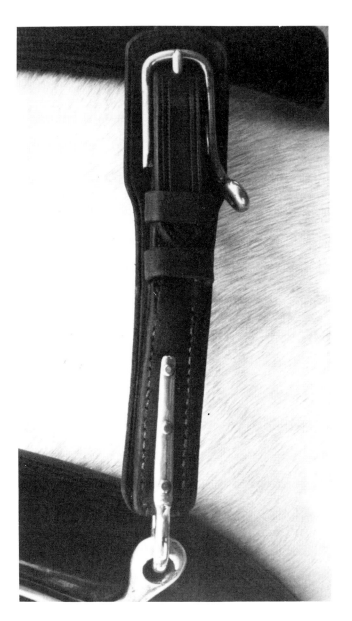

Tug buckle with eye for attachment of lead trace.

2(4) Randem

The shaft horse of a randem should always wear full collar harness. As in the case of a tandem, he should wear a breeching. The lead horse also wears a full collar. Both the lead horse and the centre horse are attached either by means of light bars (tandem bars) which clip on to the collar as well as the traces, or by means of long traces attached directly to those of the horse behind. The latter system is not recommended because the traces hang down very low and the horse may get a foot over a trace, especially when turning.

With a randem, the lead reins are 10m long. A suitable vehicle for driving a randem is a tandem cart.

2(5) Unicorn

All three horses in a unicorn should wear the same type of harness. The horse in front of the pair (the leader) should be attached to a light lead bar hooked on to the pole. Tandem lead reins may be used for the leader and passed through terrets on the inside of the wheelers' bridles.

3. Driving Teams, Tandems, etc (Driving with Four or Six Reins)

To be able to control a team, the whip must first be able to drive a single or pair safely. What has been said about driving pairs also applies on the whole to teams, and serves as a basis for team and tandem driving.

The fundamental rule that the reins must never be allowed to slide through the driver's hand is of particular importance with teams, tandems, etc. Also, if the driver has not learned, while driving a pair, to keep his left thumb and forefinger free, he will not now be able to use them independently from the other three fingers, and will not be able to adopt promptly the various rein holds used when driving with four or more reins.

If the driver has not practised, on the driving apparatus, making delicate adjustments to the length of the four or six individual reins, when he drives his team tandem or six-in-hand random, he will not be in a position to line up the leaders exactly with the wheelers or vice versa, or to regulate the distribution of the work. This, however, is essential for the driver if he wishes to drive his team correctly and properly aligned.

Driving is not just a matter of using horses for transport. It should be considered as an art, the aim of which is to bring the horses to a high level of schooling. The driver should not merely try to make the horses' task of pulling the vehicle as easy as possible. The foremost aim is to produce horses who are obedient; who 'let the aids through' without resistance (*Durchlässigkeit*); who move with elastic impulsion and swinging backs (*Schwung*), correctly set up (more or less collected depending on the situation) and with correct lateral flexion, and who yield at the poll and in the mouth, so that the driver feels

164

in harmony with them, and that he and the horses are 'pulling together' as it were.

This harmony is a particularly praiseworthy achievement in driving, because a driver does not have such close contact with his horses as a rider, and there are fewer kinds of aids which he can use. The only means the driver has at his disposal are his hands (soft, resisting or yielding, and the different rein holds) and, if need be, his whip. Driving, particularly with teams, tandems, etc, requires intelligence and quick reactions.

3(1) Putting To and Taking Out a Team

The same procedure is used for harnessing up as with a pair, except that a bridle terret is attached to the outside of the throatlatch on each of the wheelers. First, the wheelers are put to in the same way as that described for pairs. Second, the leaders are stood in front of the wheelers. Their reins are passed through the wheelers' bridle terrets, and then through the terrets on their pads. Third, they are buckled together at the end and tucked under the point strap of the pad with the wheel reins.

The rest of the procedure is the same as for pairs. With horses who are inexperienced in the lead, a strap may be run from the front of one breastcollar to the other, and attached to the pole strap rings. However, this aid should be discarded once the horses are sufficiently trained. Another way of keeping the leaders together is to interlink their inside traces.

An additional safeguard against the traces coming off is a safety strap on each end of the swingle tree. When checking that the horses have been put to correctly the driver must also ensure that the strap from the crab to the end of the pole is fastened.

The horses are taken out in the reverse order to that in which they are put to. However, with a team the driver must never attempt either operation on his own: there must always be at least one assistant present.

3(2) Taking Up the Reins of a Four-in-Hand (Team)

First, almost as with the pair reins, the driver standing level with the near (left) wheeler's pad, all the reins are pulled out from under the point strap, sorted out into lead and wheel reins, and laid across the left forearm from left to right, with the lead reins nearest to the elbow and the wheel reins nearest to the wrist. The correct amount of rein is then measured out on the wheel reins, and they are transferred into the left hand, with only the middle finger between them – unlike pair reins. The right wheel rein lies between the ring finger and the middle finger, and the left wheel rein lies between the middle finger and the index finger.

The driver then establishes a contact with the leaders' mouths on the lead reins (the right lead rein in his right hand). The position of the coupling buckles cannot be used as a gauge when measuring out the lead reins in the same way that it is with the wheel reins, so the driver must judge their length by the position of the splice (the nearest one in front of his hand when he is driving). When he is standing next to the horses, the left splice should be 5cm in front of the right one (because the driver has to cross over to the right-hand side of the vehicle to sit down). Once measured out, the lead reins are transferred from the right hand to the left, with the index finger between them. The right lead rein is then lying on top of the left wheel rein between the middle finger and the index finger, and the left lead rein is on top of the index finger.

If the leaders are standing with their traces taut when the reins are taken up, the reins should be shortened by a further 10cm approximately. If they are standing right back against the bars, the reins should be lengthened by approximately 20cm. It is not a good idea to have the assistant move the horses backwards or forwards, because this invariably makes the whole team

Working position with four-in-hand reins.

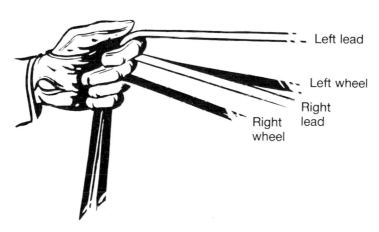

Left lead

Left wheel

Right
lead

Right
wheel

Basic position with four-in-hand reins.

167

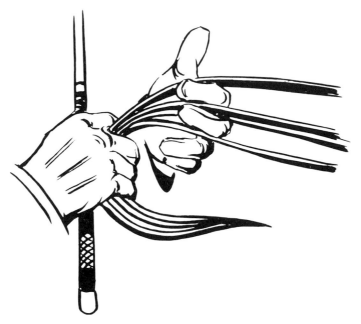

Shortening all four reins.

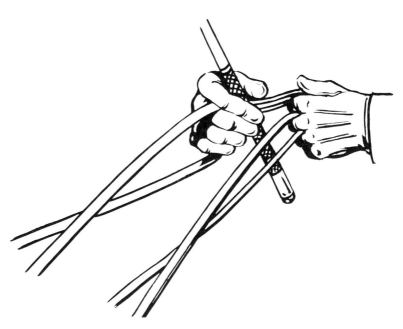

Shortening or lengthening the lead reins.

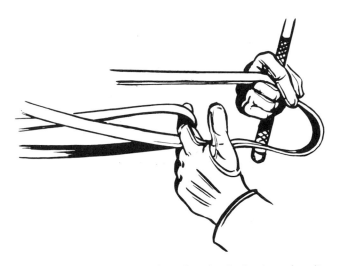

Opposition point made on the right wheel rein by looping it over the index finger. Right hand preparing to loop left lead rein under thumb. The turnout is about to begin a left turn.

restless. The amount by which all the reins need to be lengthened when the driver moves back to mount is best learnt by practice, because it depends on the construction of the vehicle. Usually, 20 to 30cm is sufficient. The method used for mounting and sitting down is the same as for pairs.

3(3) Holding the Reins of a Four-in-Hand

The reins may be held in either the basic position or the working position. The schooling position (dressage position) described for pairs and singles is not used with a team.

In the basic position all four reins remain permanently in the left hand. They must be held firmly so that they cannot be moved, except when adjusted intentionally by the right hand (for turns, etc). The lead reins are separated by the index finger and the wheel reins by the middle finger. The right lead rein lies on top of the

169

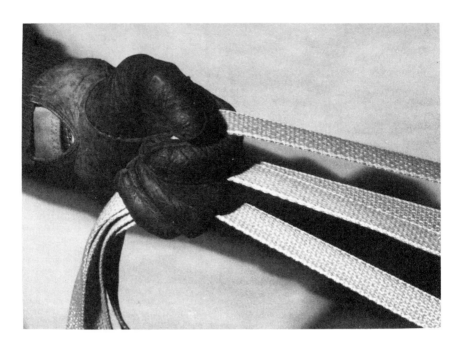

Holding the reins: basic position with four-in-hand reins.

Holding the reins: working position with four-in-hand reins.

170

left wheel rein, between the index finger and the middle finger of the driver's left hand.

In the working position the right hand, which holds the whip, is placed just in front of the left hand, with the little finger and the ring finger gripping the right reins (right wheel and right lead), and the middle finger between the two left reins. If the right hand closes on the reins, the strain is taken off the left hand without it having to be taken off the reins.

The ends of the reins hang down to the left of the driver's left thigh.

3(4) Shortening and Lengthening the Reins; Aligning the Wheelers and the Leaders in a Four-in-Hand

To lengthen all four reins by the same amount, the right hand closes on the reins in the working position, and pulls all the reins forward by the required amount through the left hand, which opens slightly to let them through. The left hand then closes again, and the right hand moves back up the reins until it is just in front of the left hand again. There are three ways of shortening all four reins simultaneously:

☐ If the adjustment to be made is only slight, the right hand slides forward up to a maximum of 5cm along the reins and closes on them in this position. The left hand then slides up to the back of the right hand. Finally both hands return to their original position (bringing the reins back with them). If the reins are still too long, the exercise may be repeated as required.

☐ If all the reins have to be shortened suddenly by a considerable amount, the driver grasps them from above, behind the left hand, with the three lower fingers of his right hand. The whip is held between the thumb and index finger of the right hand while he does so. The three lower fingers of the right hand then pull all four reins backwards through the left hand.

☐ Temporary shortening of all the reins by a large amount – e.g. when halting – is achieved by grasping the reins well forward with the right hand, and then bringing it (the right hand) back towards the body. The left hand moves upwards out of the way.

If the leaders are too much or insufficiently in draught, only the lead reins should be shortened or lengthened. Since the right lead rein lies on top of the left wheel rein (in the left hand), before the length of the lead reins is adjusted the right lead rein must first be placed on top of the index finger. To achieve this, the index finger turns outwards, comes out from between the two lead reins and is placed underneath them. The right hand is placed in front of the left, grasps the two reins, which are now lying on top of each other, and pushes them back through the left hand. If the reins need to be lengthened, instead of being pushed back they are pulled forward. When the adjustment is complete the index finger returns to its position between the two lead reins. During the adjustment, while the lead reins are being pulled forwards or pushed backwards, the wheel reins must be held firmly by the three lower fingers of the left hand to ensure that they do not alter in length.

To shorten the two wheel reins, the following method is used: first, all four reins are shortened by the method described above, then the lead reins are lengthened. To lengthen the wheel reins, the reverse method is used: all the reins are lengthened then the lead reins are shortened by the method described.

Shortening the two wheel reins on their own would result in altering the length of the lead reins and would thus cause the team to pull unevenly. This problem can also arise when shortening and lengthening individual reins. Because the right lead rein and the left wheel rein lie on top of each other between the index finger and the middle finger, these reins should never be adjusted individually.

The left lead rein and the right wheel rein are lengthened or shortened from the working position, as with pair reins, by turning the right wrist clockwise (the top of the hand forwards and downwards) or anti-clockwise (top of the hand backwards). However, if the right lead rein or the left wheel rein has to be lengthened on its own, both lead reins or both wheel reins should be adjusted, and then the left lead rein or right wheel rein adjusted back to its original length.

The horses are lined up by adjusting the left lead rein or the right wheel rein only. To move the leaders over more to the right, the right thumb and index finger, assisted by the left thumb, pull the left lead rein out further through the left hand. To position the leaders more to the left, the rein is pushed back.

If the wheelers are too far over to the right, the bottom two fingers of the right hand pull the right wheel rein out a few centimetres through the left hand, while the thumb, index finger and middle finger of the right hand keep a firm hold on the other three reins. If the wheelers are too far over to the left, the right wrist is turned so that the ring finger and little finger of the right hand can take hold of the right lead rein a little way out and push it backwards, as has been described in the section on pair driving.

Individual reins must never be pulled back through the left hand from behind as a means of lining the horses up.

3(5) Turns with a Four-in-Hand*

When turning with a four-on-hand the driver must always pay the utmost attention to the traffic or, if driving on an exercise area, to other users such as pedestrians, riders or drivers. Traffic regulations must be strictly adhered to. When driving in traffic, the relevant signals must be given, by the passenger if necessary. As

* Some references are specifically for manoeuvres made when driving on the right-hand side of the road; though see *Turns*, Basic Observations (pages 84-85).

with a pair, a left-hand turn (corner) is driven as a wide turn, and a right hand turn as a tight turn. When coming into a left turn the tempo of the trot should be slowed down. The exact speed depends on how wide the turn is and what the ground surface is like. Right-hand turns are always driven at a walk.

To *pull out or cross over to the left*, the right hand takes hold of the left lead and wheel reins some 15cm in front of the left hand, with the middle finger separating them. The left hand moves under the right, and so yields the right reins. To remain halted on the left-hand side of the road, the driver puts the two left reins across the base of his left thumb (below the thumb) and transfers the whip to the left hand so as to leave the right hand free to operate the brake. If there is too much pressure on the left reins, the left hand may be moved over to the left, or if there is not enough, and the action needs to be reinforced, the hand may move slightly to the right.

To *pull over* quickly *to the right*, leaders and wheelers need to incline simultaneously to the right. With his right hand the driver places the right wheel rein over the top of the index finger of the left hand. The right hand takes hold of both right reins together and 'takes' with the reins as much as is necessary to get the team to move over to the right. At the same time the left hand yields by turning clockwise.

When driving turns with a team, the wheelers must not be in draught. If the leaders are pulling the vehicle, or helping to do so, the corner will be cut, and the turn will be incorrect. It is the wheelers who keep the vehicle on the correct course, and the leaders must not be allowed to prevent them doing so by pulling it in another direction. In the actual turn, the inside wheeler should seem to be trying to push his way in between the two leaders.

To make a *left-hand turn* (corner) the driver slows down, applies the brake, ensures that the road is clear and signals before beginning the turn. As the leaders start to turn, they pull the pole over to the left even if they are not in draught, because the weight of the lead bars and traces is enough to bring this about. The driver must try to counter this tendency as far as possible, because otherwise he will cut the corner. The turn has only been driven correctly if the wheelers follow exactly in the tracks of the leaders throughout, and do not veer off to the left.

The driver can prevent the pole being pulled over sideways prematurely by putting the inside wheeler (in this case the left wheeler) more into draught. To achieve this, the index finger of the left hand moves outwards slightly and the right hand places the right wheel rein over the top of it. This is called 'making an opposition point on the index finger'.

When the leaders' heads have reached the point where the turn is to begin, the driver takes hold of the left lead rein between the index finger and the middle finger of the right hand at a point about 15 to 20cm in front of the left hand, feels the horses' mouths (squeezes the reins), and then makes a loop with this rein underneath the thumb of the left hand. The loop should not be too small, otherwise the outside horse will not have enough room and both leaders will be pushed into the turn by the outside trace.

With horses who are not used to being driven as a team, the opposition point on the index finger may be omitted to start with, because the wheelers will not yet have developed a tendency to cut the corner. It may even be necessary sometimes to ask them to turn, in the same way that one does the leaders.

If, after the loop has been made, the horses turn too sharply (to the left), the driver takes hold of the two right reins with his right hand and counteracts this tendency. At the same time the left hand yields by turning clockwise, but without releasing the loop. Not until both leaders and wheelers have struck off in the new direction does the driver let the loop slip slowly through his fingers. He can then also release the opposition point. Loops which are too small, or which are released too soon, are the reason for the leaders falling into the turn with their heads facing outwards, and for their being pushed into the turn by the outside lead traces against their hind legs. The loop on the left rein should therefore be released quite late to prevent the horses looking outwards (going with the wrong bend) and hanging on to the outside rein.

For a *right-hand turn* (corner) the turnout should always be brought back to a walk and the reins shortened. The wheelers must follow the leaders exactly, otherwise the turnout will cut the corner instead of describing an arc around it. If the wheelers are too far over to the right, it is essential to lengthen the right wheel rein.

When the leaders' heads reach the point where the turn begins, the driver makes a loop of approximately 20cm in the right lead rein and places it underneath his left index finger. The left hand is also moved well over to the right ('into the turn'), which prevents the wheelers turning too early. If, in spite of this, the vehicle does not go into the corner correctly, the driver takes hold of the two left reins with his right hand, at a point approximately 15cm in front of the left hand, and with his middle finger between them, and assists in the turn. The left hand yields by moving underneath the right, but without releasing the loop. Not until the vehicle is turning the corner does the driver let the loop slip through his fingers. The loop is released slightly earlier in a right-hand turn than in a left.

A right (off) wheeler who tends to throw himself into the turn may be corrected by energetic use of the whip. In such cases, an opposition point should be made with both left reins by placing them over the left thumb. The right wheeler must then be kept well up to his work and made to pull the vehicle through the corner.

In *U turns* (about turns) a small half circle is described.

For this reason the turnout must first be brought back almost to a halt. The tighter the turn, the more the horses must cross their legs. They must be made to do so with slow, controlled steps to lessen the risk of treads. To achieve this, the driver should keep a good contact on the two outside reins.

In a *left U turn* the first step is to make an opposition point on the right wheel rein by placing it on top of the index finger. Then a loop is made, as in a simple left turn (corner). However, as soon as the horses have started to turn, a second loop the same size as the first is made. Since once the leaders have turned the wheelers must also turn sharp left, the opposition point on the right wheel rein, which was made before the turn was commenced, must be released earlier than in the simple turn (corner). Usually it is released at the same time as the second loop is made. The loops are allowed to slip slowly out when the leaders have struck off in the new direction.

What has been said about left U turns also applies to *right U turns* (about turns).

Since in a right U turn the reins become longer, because the driver is sitting on the right of the vehicle, all the reins must be shortened significantly before the turn commences.

In the right U turn, as in the left, a second loop is made in the lead rein and placed under the index finger of the left hand. To prevent the horses turning prematurely, the left hand is moved over 'into the turn' – see *right-hand turn (corner)*. The turn is obtained by taking hold of both right reins with the right hand, which is then turned so that the fingernails are uppermost. This gives well-defined right-hand flexion. The left hand yields by turning clockwise and by moving 'out of the bend', but not too far, because the driver needs to keep a good contact on the outside reins and to drive the horses slowly through the turn. To straighten up at the end of the turn, the same procedure applies as for simple turns (corners):

the loops in the lead reins are allowed to slip out gradually so that the horses go straight ahead in the new direction once the turn is completed.

3(6) Rein-Back

To achieve a smooth rein-back with a team, thorough practice is necessary with pairs. Before reining back, all four reins must be shortened. The driver then brings his hands back as far as is necessary to get the horses to step backwards with even strides. Care must be taken to ensure that they do not deviate from a straight line. When he wants the horses to go forwards again, the driver moves his hand forward again in the direction of the horses' mouths and lengthens the reins. It is a good idea to apply the brake on completion of the rein-back.

To rein back to the right (or left), first a loop is made in the right (or left) rein, then the pole is pointed in the appropriate direction and the horses are asked to rein back by shortening the reins and bringing the hands back ('taking' rein). The loop in the reins remains and the pole stays at an angle until the vehicle is in the desired position. The turnout is then halted and the loop in the reins released.

3(7) The Team Whip and its Use

The driver of a four-in-hand must be in a position to give the necessary whip aids to the leaders as well as to the wheelers. For him to be able to do so, the whip must be correctly constructed of the correct materials, and must be the right length. Furthermore, the driver must be practised in using it. Early practice with the whip is best done on a dummy horse in front of the vehicle.

So that it does not become caught in the wheels, annoy passers-by or upset the other horses in the team, the thong of a four-in-hand whip must be caught and wound round the stick when it is not being used on the leaders.

Catching the thong is easier if the stick is fairly stiff and has knots on the top part, on which the thong can gain purchase. The thong, which consists of a strip of leather with a lash at the end, must be firm and substantial. (See *The driving whip and its application.*) The thong is caught by describing an 'S' shape in the air with it, as shown in the drawing on page 104.

When the driver is on the box the thong should be thrown and caught to the right of the vehicle, low down and slightly to the front, so that it does not become caught on trees or traffic signs. Even when practising without the horses, the driver should sit fairly high up so that he can learn to do this correctly. When the thong has been caught and furled, the end of the thong is held under the thumb, and the loop hanging down from the top end of the stick – the 'double thong', as it is called – serves as a whip for the wheelers.

To use the whip on the leaders, the driver first unwinds the thong by swinging the whip round while pointing it downwards, forwards and to the right. He then releases the end of the thong from underneath his thumb and moves his hand down to the bottom of the handpiece by pushing the whip through his hand with his right thigh.

To use the whip on the right (off) leader, the driver describes a clockwise circular movement with his arm. The whole of the arm from the shoulder joint is used, and the whip laid on the horse as far forward as possible, in an upwards movement. (If possible the horse should be hit on the belly just behind the pad.) To use the whip on the left (near) leader, the driver flicks the thong over to the left of the horses with a slight twist of his wrist (taking care not to disturb them). He then describes a circle anti-clockwise with a swinging movement of his whole arm, and lays the thong well forward on the left leader.

The thong should not be pulled straight back, which would cause it to disturb the wheelers. If, as he brings the thong back, the driver turns the bow of the whip slowly from left to right above the horses, the thong will fall on to his right thigh or under his right arm. It can then be picked up with the thumb and index finger of the right hand and held against the stick. The right hand then moves over to the left and the left thumb pulls the thong through the right hand (taking care to keep the reins exactly as they were) until the end is reached. The double thong can then be caught.

When giving whip aids, the whole arm must always be used. If the driver uses only his wrist, which is incorrect, the thong will tend to become caught on the harness or on overhanging trees when he tries to bring it back after using it on the leaders.

3(8) Tandem and Unicorn

The same rein holds and positions which are used when driving a four-in-hand are also used with tandems and unicorns, though scaled to their particular requirements. However, tandem driving presents particular problems because the reins are much closer together, and the driver cannot tell so easily, by looking at them, which rein is which. For this reason, in addition to the four-in-hand rein holds, there are two extra holds (the so-called 'tandem holds') which are worthy of mention, and which help to prevent the reins being confused.

For a *left turn*, from the working position the right hand releases the left reins and slides 10cm forward on the right reins. The two right reins are held as one, and the driver picks up the left lead rein with the thumb and index finger of the right hand and loops it for the left-hand turn. The loop must be made in several stages, and the left thumb should not be allowed to come in front of the right thumb.

For a *right turn*, both lead reins must be shortened: the leader cannot pull the vehicle round if the traces are slack. The driver takes hold of all four reins with his right hand, about 15cm in front of his left hand, and

180

then releases the left lead rein and increases his hold on the left wheel rein. He turns his left hand anti-clockwise and moves it slightly forwards in a yielding action. This lengthens the left lead and the leader turns to the right.

Feeling the horses' mouths to prepare them for the turn is even more important in tandem driving than in four- or six-in-hand driving. If it is neglected the leader may spin round to face the driver.

Driving a tandem is considerably easier if the correct type of harness is used. Long traces of the sort which are attached directly to the wheeler's harness, and not to bars, have the disadvantage that the leader pulls the vehicle sideways across the turn if the driver does not shorten the lead reins sufficiently beforehand. Moreover, there is a risk that when the traces are too slack, the leader could get a leg over them. It is better to use double bars (tandem bars) to attach the traces to, though they do have one slight disadvantage: the wheeler tends to have to carry them on his neck, and they bang against his forelegs when going down hills.

3(9) Driving a Six-in-Hand and a Random

The best way to hold the reins with a six-in-hand is the same as with a four-in-hand, but with the addition of an extra pair of reins, those of the leaders. The lead reins of a six-in-hand lie on top of those of the swing pair, i.e. left lead lies on top of left swing and right lead lies on top of right swing. Underneath right swing lies left wheel, and below these, on its own, is right wheel.

With six horses in front of him the driver must be constantly on the lookout. He must be able to 'see' whether the horses are correctly aligned and whether the lead and swing horses are sufficiently 'in work' to make the traces taut, but no more. Under no circumstances must the leaders and swing pair pull the vehicle unless extra traction is required, for example when going uphill, or in heavy going.

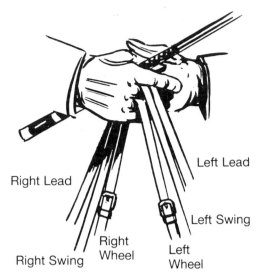

The position of the reins in a six-in-hand.

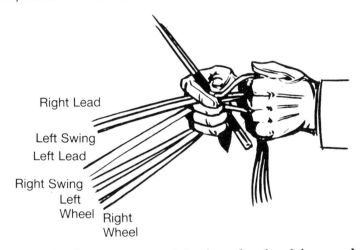

If the *leaders are too much in draught,* the driver makes a small loop in each of the lead reins at the back of the left hand and then lets it fall free behind his hand.*

If the *swing pair is too much in draught,* the driver puts his index finger underneath the top four reins, shortens them as for a four-in-hand, replaces his index finger in the original position and lengthens the lead reins again.

---

* This method of shortening the lead reins is described in more detail in Chapter 6 of Tom Ryder's *On the Box Seat.*

If the *leaders are insufficiently in draught*, the lead reins are pulled forward individually through the left hand to lengthen them.

If the *swing pair is insufficiently in draught*, the lead and swing reins are lengthened, and then the lead reins are shortened up again.

It is up to the driver to decide whether or not the whip should be used.

In a *right turn* (corner) it is particularly important that the right (off) wheeler is going well into his traces, and that he pulls the vehicle into and through the turn. The driver can prepare for the turn by lengthening the right wheel rein by one or two centimetres beforehand. Since the lead and swing reins lie on top of each other, it is not always easy to manipulate the lead reins correctly. Placing the right lead rein on top of the left index finger beforehand will make it easier to get hold of, and prevent it becoming caught up with the other reins.

To begin the turn, the right hand makes a sufficiently large loop in the right lead rein and places it underneath the left index finger. Then, immediately, a loop is made in the right swing rein, and another (second) one in the right lead rein. When looping ('pointing') the reins, the left hand moves 'into the turn', that is, towards the driver's right hip, to prevent the wheelers turning too soon and the leaders falling into the turn. The loops are released after the turn as required, with the right hand assisting. Since right-hand turns are always driven at a walk, the reins need to be shortened beforehand. On completion of the turn, they are lengthened again.

To make a *left turn*, the driver first performs a half-halt to get the horses sufficiently collected. The reins are then lengthened slightly, depending on the size of the turn, and the left lead rein is placed on top of the left thumb. This will prevent the swing rein being picked up with it on the turn. A preliminary loop is made in the left lead rein and placed under the thumb. Then a second loop is made with the left lead rein and the left swing rein.

On completion of the turn, the loops are allowed to slip out, assisted by the right hand. Before and during the turn, the inside (left) wheeler should be sent forward as required with a correctly placed whip aid to make him pull the vehicle correctly through the turn.

All turns with a six-in-hand depend on the reins being held absolutely securely in the left hand, and the loops being made correctly. Once one pair has struck off in the new direction, the driver should tend to drive the pair behind as if he were trying to send them in between the horses in front. With a six-in-hand the problem of the wheelers making the vehicle cut the corner does not arise to the same extent as it does with a four-in-hand because the swing pole provides a certain amount of resistance to the main pole. However, the driver must still keep a good contact on the outside reins, though without preventing the horses from bending correctly to the inside on the turn.

With a *random* the reins are held and handled as for a six-in-hand. The lead reins must be handled with great sensitivity, but positively. It is very rare to find an absolutely steady leader who will go forwards and straight without another horse next to him, and who will obey the driver's rein aids without hesitation.

3(10) Faults in Team and Tandem Driving

All faults which occur in pair driving also occur when driving teams, tandems, etc, where they become more significant.

Failing to take up the reins correctly is a particularly bad fault in team driving, because when the horses move off they are not in line or equally in work.

If the driver does not hold the reins securely in his left hand, and lets one rein or another slip, the whole team will soon become unsettled and will not be properly under control.

If the brake is not used at the right time, the lead

bars may bang against the leaders' hind legs, causing them to kick or bolt. The driver of a team (or tandem) must be absolutely familiar with the handling of a team (or tandem) whip. Whips hanging down get in the way, inconvenience other road users, and can even cause an accident. If the driver is not skilled in using the whip on the leaders, he catches the wheelers with it and unsettles them, while the leaders hang back.

A common fault is too long lead (and swing) reins. The leaders (and swing pair) are then too much in draught and the driver not properly in control of his team.

Index

Index

Index